CITY
BUILDERS

CITY BUILDERS

THE MALEKS, THE OLYMPICS, AND A HISTORIC GIFT TO VANCOUVER

RICHARD LITTLEMORE

BARLOW
BOOKS

Jacket image: Millennium's Olympic Village Community, Vancouver, BC

Canada's first LEED Platinum community, covering 25 acres over 8 city blocks with 9 acres of parkland, 21 multi-storey buildings, and 70,000 square feet of retail space, including Urban Fare, London Drugs, Terra Breads, TD Canada Trust, and the Legacy store. The development, designed and built by Millennium in a record 30 months, served as the Athlete's Village for the 2010 Winter Olympic Games, providing housing and amenities for over 2,800 athletes and officials during this historic event. It is considered by many to be one of the finest communities in the world, from an ecological and architectural perspective.

Main text copyright © Peter and Shahram Malek, 2024

Library and Archives Canada Cataloguing in Publication data available upon request.

978-1-998841-04-2 (hardcover)

Printed in Canada

Publisher: Sarah Scott
Book producer: Tracy Bordian/At Large Editorial Services
Cover design: Paul Hodgson
Interior design and layout: Ruth Dwight
Copy editing: Eleanor Gasparik
Proofreading: Rhiannon Thomas
Indexing: Audrey Dorsch

For more information, visit **www.barlowbooks.com**

Barlow Book Publishing Inc.
96 Elm Avenue, Toronto, ON
M4W 1P2 Canada

For Amir and Mahin Malek, who invested their hope in their children and who gave us all the gifts we could ever have wanted to face the world

—PETER AND SHAHRAM MALEK

Contents

THE MALEKS OF YAZD

Through their long history in Iran, the Malek family was known and addressed generally by the surname Malekzadeh, but in formal documents, the name appeared as Malekyazdi, indicating that the family originally hailed from the city of Yazd. That formal designation carried over when the family left Iran, and patriarch Amir Malekyazdi used it during his time in France. In Canada, however, the next generation returned to the original Malek. While all those derivations may appear in formal and informal accounts, this book uses Malek in most references.

FOREWORD

By Larry Beasley, C.M.

Peter and Shahram Malek have been key players in Vancouver's development scene for as long as I can remember. I met them in the early 1990s, in my role as deputy planner in the City of Vancouver, and when I graduated to co-director of planning, I came to know them as vital contributors to a world-changing endeavour. It was a transformational time in a city that has come to exemplify some of the best elements of contemporary, liveable, sustainable, and resilient urbanism. I'm proud that people the world over now talk about "Vancouverism"—we clearly did a lot of things right, as I describe in my own book of the same name.

The period of Vancouver's transformation was as frenetic as it was innovative. New ideas about city living and development were coming from every direction—some great, others not as well thought out. A lot of money was at stake, but so was the quality of Vancouver's neighbourhood life; tensions and emotions could get pretty high. So, it was often a challenge to negotiate with developers, and with anxious citizens and advocacy organizations. I would try to meet out-side the conference room for coffee or lunch to cool the ardour and to build trust for a more considered discussion. In contrast to many of these encounters, any meeting with the Maleks was a distinct plea-sure. They always started the dialogue early in their process, so they could learn about the City's concerns and build solutions into their projects from the beginning. I soon found that I could depend on them to bring something interesting, and to be completely open to suggestions that would help us achieve public as well as private objec-tives. As developers, as people, they just had this optimistic sense that they were always going to find a way forward. Shahram had that quiet, thoughtful approach, and Peter so often brought in essential new content that would shift the direction for the better. In a world where too many people feel they can claim victory only when some-one else loses, Peter and Shahram seemed to always be looking for the win/win. They brought insight, a broad world view, and a sincere concern for the public good. And because they offered wisdom that I could learn from, beyond the needs of the moment, I started to look forward to our meetings, knowing I would take away more than you would usually expect.

Even before I got to know the Maleks socially, I appreciated each of them as solid individuals and, together, as a thoughtful force in our community. I respected their approach, and I admired their work. As I got to know them on a more personal level, I also learned more about their story. I learned that, as immigrants whose family had con-trolled one of the biggest construction and development firms in Iran, they had been driven from their homeland and had arrived in Vancouver in the early 1980s—starting from scratch. I learned about the family ethic of a strong education. I learned about parents who Peter and Shahram looked up to as smart contributors, especially their father for his business acumen and his unstaunchable tenacity, even in the face of deplorable circumstances and barriers. I learned how two brothers of very different style and temperament could balance one another in an enviable and unique partnership of business and family responsibility. I saw their resilience and their courage. Even in the most difficult circumstances, they just carried on.

I left the City of Vancouver in 2006 and spent a good part of the next five years leading a planning initiative in the Emirate of Abu Dhabi, and also traveling the world on other projects. I saw much to broaden my perspective, including the fascinations of very different religious and social frameworks. On my trips back to Vancouver, I observed how much the brothers' inherited grit was in evidence as they executed their largest project ever: a complete neighbourhood in one of Vancouver's most valuable and high-profile locations. It was a pivotal development because it would also serve as the athletes' village for the 2010 Olympic Winter Games. It was also a massive success—an unprecedented achievement. In the process, however, the Maleks got caught in a global economic meltdown and a local political showdown; even having delivered the project in beautiful condition and ahead of their Olympic deadline, they suffered economic injuries and a personal toll all but equal to the devastation they endured in revolutionary Iran. Their subsequent recovery, and their continuing contribution, is all the more remarkable for the obstacles others tried to put in their way.

I was thinking about all this some years ago, and when I ran into the brothers at a local development industry event, I shared my thoughts. I said there are lots of really good accounts by architects and planners who have documented this important part of Vancouver's history, but hardly any books by developers. And even among those, there are few people who have such a compelling personal and family saga. I told them I saw it as a classic Canadian tale of a new world, new adventures, and new opportunity, and I urged them to put their story down on paper, to write their own book. Peter and Shahram thanked me warmly—they are unfailingly polite—but the moment passed. They seemed more interested when I brought it up again the next time I saw them, but they were still unmoved. By the third meeting, in a catch-up lunch just before Christmas in 2019, I was beginning to think that they were simply overwhelmed by the prospect of wrestling such a sprawling chronicle onto the page. So, I offered to introduce them to Richard Littlemore, a writer I knew to have the experience, the background, and the collaborative spirit necessary to do the story justice.

It's obvious now that Peter and Shahram accepted the introduction and found in Richard someone who could make the whole process not just manageable but enjoyable. And I am delighted with the results, now available for all to read. This is a story that begged to be told. It is a family story, an immigrant story, a development story, and a political story. It's an adventure story, even a story of redemption. But most especially, it's a story of two men who, with integrity, honour, and amazing resilience, have contributed immeasurably to the building of what I am again proud to say is an exemplary city. They have given us much for which to be grateful, not least in sharing this compelling piece of personal, corporate, and civic history.

CITY
BUILDERS

I hope that my children and their descendants, now scattered around the world, far from their homeland, can learn to battle life's difficulties with strength of character. I hope that they come to treat defeats as learning opportunities and use setbacks to fortify themselves against future challenges. I hope that wherever in the world they live, they never forget their ancestral homeland, and prove to the people of their adopted countries that they have brought with them such gifts of resourcefulness, creativity, love, and determination that will guarantee their prosperity and their welcome wherever they may go.

—AMIR MALEK

In the tradition of our parents, Amir and Mahin Malek, who asked much but always gave more, we offer this book as evidence of our own effort and as encouragement to a new generation. To our beloved children, from Peter, Roxanna, Tara, and Persia, and from Shahram, Nader, Alex, and Nina, we echo our father's words: be resourceful, creative, loving and determined—be resilient—and more than merely prosper, you will be welcome citizens of the world.

—PETER AND SHAHRAM MALEK

A GIFT TO THE CITY

I t's one of the oldest conventions in literature: every great story needs a crisis, a dark moment from which the hero (or heroes!) can rise in triumph. And this is one such tale—a story of two brothers who were targeted, displaced, and summarily stripped of their wealth, who came to Canada with little more than their own energy and ambition, to rebuild a fortune and redeem an admired family name. But for Peter and Shahram Malek, who left Tehran in the shattering aftermath of the 1979 Iranian Revolution, the story was destined to have two bad beats. Because here, after three decades of building one of Vancouver's most successful real estate development companies—and after executing one of the most complex and high-profile projects in the city's history—they ran headlong into another implacable government, one that showed equal indifference to their contribution and that stripped them once more, this time in a way that seemed even more purposeful and more personal.

The story still ends well. The Maleks bounced back. They are again doing work that any city would applaud. But, as in every great narrative, if you're looking for evidence of resilience—if you're looking for character—the crisis is probably the best place to start. There's nothing like a scene of comprehensive economic ruin to focus the mind.

IT'S APRIL 2011, and Shahram Malek has just walked into the expansive boardroom of Farris LLP, the high-tone law firm that the City of Vancouver uses when some legal task is too big to manage in-house. Arrayed down the long table is an orderly row of yellow, letter-sized folders, all standing neatly in clear plastic hangers. It must have taken some hyper-organized legal assistant hours just to bring in the files, arrange them correctly, and stand them up in this temporary location. Shahram is so struck by the sight that he stops, takes out his BlackBerry, and snaps a photo, as if this is something that he actually wants to remember.

The resulting image—grainy and badly lit—offers no hint of the content of the folders. But you can glean some clue of their import from the countenance of Shahram's brother, Peter, who is sitting to one side. He is distraught. Deflated. He has the detached look of someone standing before a firing squad. As well he might. This row of folders represents pretty much everything that he and Shahram own, and it is imminently at risk. Here are the titles to thirty-two properties in Vancouver, Burnaby, North Vancouver, and Toronto, representing tens of millions of dollars in hard assets and hundreds of millions in presumed value—virtually everything they have assembled in decades of building their Millennium Development Group. And the Maleks have been summoned this day to sign the whole fortune over to the City of Vancouver, for which gesture they will leave without receiving so much as a handshake in return.

All this could play as a willful act of financial violence—of ruthless vengeance and unrestrained political opportunism. But that implies an unsavoury motive, what the lawyers call malice aforethought. Whereas the bureaucrats and politicians who precipitated this moment would say what people always say in these circumstances: it's nothing personal. Which is—as it always is—ridiculous. If you're the person being run over by a bus, of course it's personal.

The bewildering part—the heartbreaking part—emerges when you ask what the Maleks did to deserve such treatment. For, surely, no one is ceremoniously stripped of their every asset without having triggered the defenestration by some bad act. But here's the truth, an article of historical fact on which even the Maleks' worst critics will agree: in the course of incurring the City's ire, the brothers built Vancouver's most beautiful, most sustainable, and, ultimately, most successful new neighbourhood: Olympic Village, celebrated as the first LEED Platinum-certified community in North America. In the process, and against a preposterous timeline, they also provided the 2010 Olympics with what all agreed was the best athletes' village in the history of the Games, and they did it on time and (they will argue) on budget.

Unfortunately, they did all this during the biggest global economic meltdown in a century and—worse!—in the midst of a municipal election in which they became the practice bag in a political punch-up. For their part, the brothers never even stepped into the ring. They kept their heads down and did what they had promised to do. But when the fight ended, it was the Maleks who had taken the worst blows. Despite the timely completion of the neighbourhood and the success of the Olympic Games, at the first hint of a shortfall, the City of Vancouver—the Maleks' client and their financier—pushed the project into receivership and ordered City lawyers to seize every asset,

every scrap of equity attached to the corporate and personal guaran-
tees the Maleks had provided along the way.

Which brings us back to the boardroom, the row of files, the box of
pens at the ready lest any obstacle slow down the signing. This is the
City's bounty. This is the moment when the brothers have been summoned to sign over everything they have built, earned, or acquired in
their remarkably productive lifetimes.

When the signing is over, Peter and Shahram withdraw for a debrief
in the nearby office of one of the city's leading real estate lawyers, Neil
Kornfeld. It would be hard to imagine these as men who would weep;
they're from a background more likely to show emotion by lingering, briefly, over a firm handshake. But contemplating the now-empty
space where their wealth had been, and feeling humiliated, Peter and
Shahram start talking about another crisis—an earlier moment when
the Malek family lost everything. Their father, Amir Malek, had an
enormously successful career in Iran, with a business he started from
scratch in the late 1940s. His Armeh Construction Company built
roads, bridges, tunnels, airports, whole townships, and an entire
Olympic-calibre sports complex.

But that triumph also ended abruptly, amid the gunfire and Islamic
fervour of the 1979 Iranian Revolution. Under gathering threat, the
Maleks left the country with nothing more than what they could fit
in a suitcase. Sitting now in Kornfeld's office, one of the brothers says
what they both are thinking: "It's just the same. We are starting, again,
with nothing."

Kornfeld, apparently more pragmatic than diplomatic, waves
off the comparison. He points out that when the Maleks came to
Canada, they were unknown, but they had excellent references, so lots
of people were willing to finance their work. Whereas now, Kornfeld
says, thanks to the controversy, thanks to the toxic publicity attached

to this moment, "Everyone knows who you are and no one will lend you money."

WHATEVER YOUR AGE, there are times in life when the best shoulder you can seek, for comfort or consolation, is your mother's, so it's fortunate on this day that Peter and Shahram's mother, Mahin Malek, is visiting from Paris. Father Amir had been wary of this complicated Olympic deal from the outset, often questioning whether the City could be trusted and urging his sons to take a harder line. Now that the City has made its play, now that Peter and Shahram have paid such a high price, they might well have expected someone to say, "I told you so." But Mahin is not that sort. Seeing her sons brood, hearing them worry aloud about losing the project—about sacrificing everything— she shrugs and says, don't worry.

She says: "Just think of it as a gift to the city."

BLESSINGS: THE EARLY YEARS

It's hard to pinpoint the origin of a buoyant spirit. It's hard to explain why someone, in comfort or adversity, would choose always to search out the best characterization of their circumstance—to find the good in every situation and, within reason, in other people. It can be tempting to attribute an optimistic outlook to a comfortable and supportive upbringing. But the record shows that privileged children are just as likely to be self-centred and entitled as they are to be generous and grateful. Affluence and social advantage are no guarantee of resilience or strength of character, nor of kindness or integrity. There is something more, perhaps something that is sourced in a genetic predisposition, but most certainly something that must have been nurtured.

Peter and Shahram Malek have that spirit. They have revelled in good times and bounced back in bad. They have sought justice for others as well as themselves, and to hear them tell their story, they have found, again and again, sometimes in the unlikeliest moments, that the world is filled with (Shahram's favourite phrase) "very nice people."

Certainly, there was much for which to be grateful in their birthplace, Tehran, in the 1950s. Their father, Amir Malek, started his own firm, Armeh Construction, in 1946, after graduating as a civil engineer from the University of Charlottenburg in wartime Berlin. The Armeh Construction Company became an immediate success through ingenuity and old-fashioned hard work.

Amir was busy, well able to provide, and devoted to family. As Peter describes it, even in those early days, the Maleks lived very close to downtown Tehran in "a nice house, with a garden and a swimming pool." And each summer, they rented a villa in the hills, 60 kilometres to the east—away from the heat of the city. The family celebrated the season as Amir commuted, sometimes every day, in and out of Tehran.

As a father—and a man of his time—Amir was both strict and indulgent. He didn't let his children take their privileged environment for granted. And he refused to let them trifle with unhealthy drinks like Coca-Cola! But he regularly let Peter go off to stay with a favourite aunt, in Isfahan, where, Peter says, "I was totally free. I could drink as much Coke as I wanted!"

The boys remember an epic vacation on which the whole family, including their one-year-old sister, Marjan, flew from Tehran to Beirut, which was then a beautiful and peaceful city known as "the Paris of the Middle East"—the kind of place you could buy shiny things that weren't so readily available in Iran. Amir bought a brand-new Ford Fairlane and set out on a Middle Eastern tour, driving the family first into Syria for a visit to Damascus and then east to Iraq. "Everything seemed so peaceful," Peter says. In Iraq, they drove to the holy Shi'ite city of Karbala, not because they were especially devout, but because it, too, was beautiful, a worthy destination on architectural as well as spiritual grounds. They went on to Baghdad for a visit with relatives and then they flew back home, the now-popular Ford following at the hands of a cousin a week later.

Two new babies came next, a second sister, Maryam, and a third, Mandana, who, heartbreakingly, was born with a congenital heart defect. It wasn't a subject much discussed around the children, but the boys, who were older, were aware of the stress and the upset. So, the timing seemed perfect when their aunt came again from Isfahan. Peter, who assumed he would be joining her on the return trip, says he went to sleep dreaming about "as much Coke as I wanted." But when he awoke the next day, he found that she was already gone. When he complained, his parents announced what they presented as an even-more-exciting plan. Rather than going to Isfahan, he and Mandana were going to join their mother and father on a trip to England. Peter remembers Amir and Mahin talking up "beautiful England, where there are lots of cars and beautiful buildings." And all the while, he was thinking, "There are cars in Tehran!"

England was, indeed, beautiful, even in the eyes of a ten-year-old. "I mean, it wasn't, 'Wow! I-want-to-stay-here-for-the-rest-of-my-life'," Peter says. But it was lovely.

But Peter quickly realized, however, that the trip was not really a holiday. They had come in hopes that a famous London surgeon might be able to help baby Mandana, which was a lost promise; she would die before the end of the year. The second revelation, which dawned on Peter more slowly, was that he would not be returning to Iran with the family. "My dad said, 'We think it's a good idea for you to go to school here.'" And while Peter made it abundantly clear that he thought it was a terrible idea, he and his parents made their way to

Charing Cross railway station, took a train to Tunbridge Wells and then a chauffeur-driven car to Langton Green, in Kent, to the prep school Holmewood House.

LOOKING BACK NOW, Peter acknowledges that the school was beautiful—and would have been more so had it not been "always raining." The main building at Holmewood is a grand Georgian neo-classical mansion designed by the great nineteenth-century English architect Decimus Burton, and the rambling additions—roughly in keeping with the original architectural theme—allowed it to keep its homey feel, even if it felt nothing like home for a ten-year-old with no friends and no useful command of the English language.

Amir and Mahin did all they could to ensure Peter was well settled. They arranged for a guardian, Mrs. Mary Wise, who would look in once in a while, provide the odd treat, and care for Peter on holidays. Amir also engaged a Farsi tutor, Mr. Bahar, so Peter would keep and develop his own language even as he learned a new one. Then mother and father got back in the car and back on the train to spend more time with Mandana and the doctors in London. When they came back to Holmewood a week or so later for a last visit before returning to Iran, Peter was inconsolable. And, it turned out, faster than the chauffeur had expected. As the driver pulled away on the gravel driveway, and Amir and Mahin turned to wave goodbye, they found that their fleet-footed son had caught up to the car, climbed up on the rear bumper, and was holding on frantically and crying desperately. Amir, Mahin, *and* the chauffeur had to get out and pry him off.

The next six months were among the most wretched in Peter's life. There were only three Farsi speakers among Holmewood's one hundred students. Two were friends of the family, Bahram Eftekhari, eight, and his younger brother, Kami, six. It was their father who had recommended the school to Amir and Mahin. The age difference created a gap that left ten-year-old Peter still feeling alone. The third boy, Hamid Yamani, was a year or two older and, at first blush, dismissive to the point of bullying. Peter's spoken English was near useless and his written English so bad that he had to copy his own name from the printed version on his school-issue handkerchief. When the teachers caught him doing so, they bumped him from the fourth form to the third, leaving him with a mercifully short-lived reputation as a big, not-very-bright new boy.

Before they left for Iran, Peter's parents had given him a sheaf of thin, blue airmail letters—single sheets that you could fill out, fold up and seal so the letter became its own envelope. Having been instructed to write weekly, Peter did so, penning long lists of complaints broken only by fervid pleas to be brought home. He also wrote side notes to Shahram, with dark details and dire warnings: "Don't come here," he wrote. "It's terrible. It's like a nightmare!" Ever the attentive father, Amir sat down with every letter, corrected the spelling and grammar, and sent it back.

But he found no peace in doing so. Every morning, while Amir was shaving, eight-year-old Shahram budged his way into the bathroom and prosecuted a long campaign. He said, again and again: "I want to be with my brother." This was the mischievous child, the boy who was known in the family for swatting his older brother and then running to his mother, to heap the blame on Peter and to claim protection. But there was never any actual enmity between them. Looking back, Shahram says, "We were close. And I was suddenly alone." It took four or five months, but Shahram persisted and, finally, Amir and Mahin surrendered. Just before his ninth birthday, they put Shahram on a plane to London, "and I was in such a rush, I didn't even say a proper goodbye." He regretted it the instant they closed the door of the aircraft, and he spent the whole journey sitting, bereft, beside his chaperone, Mr. Eftekhari (Bahram and Kami's father), who was returning to London from a visit to Tehran.

Still, Shahram was excited and impatient to see his brother. So, he was disappointed when he and Mr. Eftekhari landed in London and went first to the home of the boys' guardians, Mary and Wilfred Wise. After a lonely night, Mrs. Wise rousted him for an early morning trip to Gorringes Department Store, which you might imagine as a model for Harry Potter's Diagon Alley. It was the kind of place where new students could get everything they needed—which, for an eight-year-old schoolboy, consisted mostly of socks, short pants, and a blazer (long trousers being reserved for boys older than eleven). The Wise family were also keen riders and set off on another detour to their favourite stable in Reading to put Shahram on a horse. Galloping through the countryside, an experience he still remembers as "terrifying," Shahram longed all the more for the company of his brother.

The next morning, finally, they followed the trail to Tunbridge Wells by train from Charing Cross and then by car to Langton Green where, as Peter had frequently reported, the rain was coming down in sheets. Mrs. Shelley, the administrator, greeted the car and brought Shahram into a reception room, where she left him to wait for the much-anticipated reunion. Moments later, as Shahram was somberly looking out of the large Georgian windows onto the rain beating down on the lush green landscape, Peter burst into the room in a wave of frustration and belligerence, shouting: "What are you doing here? I told you not to come!"

Shahram accepted the wisdom of this position almost immediately and, in his first letter home, admitted his error and asked to return to Tehran. His father's response: "You're a man—and you've made your decision." Shahram persisted, pleading over another airmail appeal to leave the sodden Holmewood. When a fat tear fell from his cheek and stained the blue page, he circled it and made a note so there was no doubt where the blot came from. True to form, Amir corrected the letter and returned it by the next post, complete with an extra scolding for Shahram having mixed English and Farsi in the same letter.

THE NEXT FEW months dragged on in a wash of strange customs and boyish politics. Shahram had not previously worn a tie, much less learned to manage an appropriate knot. When Peter knotted it for him, Shahram was careful to keep it that way, slipping it on every morning before the rush to breakfast. It was probably inevitable that another student would notice and undo the tie, leaving Shahram in a panic, tracking down Peter to retie the knot!

Shahram's first nemesis was "Buster" Walls, an eight-year-old American whose real name was Ira. The boisterous Buster was all red hair and freckles, and on one of the first evenings when the boys were gathered in the school gym, he barged up to Shahram and said, "Do you want to fight!?" As in every boy's life, when the real answer is, "No!" but the result is inevitably, "Yes," Shahram soon found himself wrestling on a mat. Given the place and the time, you can only imagine this contest to have been short and strictly bound by the polite boxing rules and conventions of the Marquess of Queensberry, but it was still a bruising assault on Shahram's sense of security. Even today, however, he sounds surprised to report, "I won!" Ever generous, however, he also immediately allows that his fellow combatant might remember that detail differently. Regardless, Buster came up afterwards and announced, "You're my best friend!" And friends they were until the US Army posted Buster's officer father back to the States; even then, the boys maintained a correspondence for many years.

For Peter, the pugilistic challenge came with Hamid Yamani. Hamid was smart, cold, and derisive—if addressed in Farsi, he would answer in English, if at all. Peter found him to be "a bully and a snob," which offended Peter's sense of justice. "I was disappointed that an Iranian guy would be mean to another Iranian." So, he challenged Hamid to do battle—in that English boys' school way—and, with less surprise than Shahram, reports, first, that he, too, came out the winner and, second, that he, too, cemented a friendship that lasted all through their years at Holmewood.

It's easy to think about Holmewood and overlay the harsh images of old English boarding schools that abound in dour books and movies—the dreary days, the strict teachers, the long, lonely stretches between visits with family. Even after Shahram's arrival, the boys remained isolated from one another, segregated by age. After the affluence of their early years, they found themselves bunking two or three to a room on hard army mattresses over cold metal frames. "And the food was awful," Peter says. Shahram adds, "Kippers for breakfast. We hated being woken up by the smell of kippers!"

When the boys challenged their parents—at the time and later—about the decision to send them to such a place, Mahin answered that she and Amir wanted the boys "to be raised in a tough environment." Which included a tolerance for school food. When Shahram complained that he had found a moving slug in his salad, Mahin simply said that if his English hosts had included the slug in his meal, they must have done so for the vitamins!

IF AMIR AND Mahin sincerely hoped for a tough environment, they got what they paid for. Any infraction at Holmewood that was deemed major was punishable with "six of the best," delivered to the perpetrator's bare behind with whatever tool the disciplinarian favoured. For

Jeremy Heale, the housemaster at the Cedar House dormitory where both boys were billeted, it was a cricket bat, and while Peter can't remember what he did to earn his first beating, he remembers feeling that it was unjust. "I had to go to his study and take down my pants."

The mandatory disrobing was perfectly practical. Too many boys had shown up for discipline with everything from magazines to extra clothing tucked into their britches. Still, Peter says, "It was humiliating." For that humiliation—for the injustice more than the pain—Peter also remembers later letting the air out of the tires of Mr. Heale's Land Rover, an act of revenge for which he was never caught. Shahram also remembers getting six from Mr. Heale—for walking through the gym while chewing gum—but he recalls that the instrument of choice was a riding crop. "I think it was worse than the bat," Shahram says, "because it curled around." But there were no lasting hard feelings. On the contrary, the brothers reconnected with Jay Heale, who was living in South Africa, as adults and they expressed their gratitude for what they still consider his overwhelmingly positive influence on their young lives.

The unquestioned star of the Holmewood show was Headmaster Robert Bairamian. Far from the Dickensian image of headmaster as distant and imperious authoritarian, Shahram says that Bairamian "was a really cool guy." And the impression was unanimous, according to Haydn Keenan, an Australian filmmaker and fellow Holmewood student from this period. Keenan says that "Bob" Bairamian was "a unique alpha Silverback," whom everyone loved and who made the Holmewood experience formative and fabulous for a whole generation of boys. The grandson of refugees from the Armenian genocide, Bairamian had been born in Nicosia, Cyprus, and educated during his early years in a school run by his mother. He had come to England for "prep" and "public" schooling before doing a degree at Cambridge.

Keenan, who has been researching a documentary on Holmewood, says that during his Cambridge years, Bairamian became "more English than the English"—ever after attired in a double-breasted blazer with a silk handkerchief in the top pocket and always celebrating his short success as a Cambridge cricketer. Immediately after graduating, in 1957, Bairamian took what he imagined was a temporary teaching job at Holmewood. But two years later, when the previous headmaster committed suicide, Bairamian—still just twenty-four years old—was bumped into the top job.

He was, by all accounts, born to it. In a short film that Keenan made to celebrate Bairamian's life (he died in 2018 at age eighty-three), Bahram Eftekhari, the fellow-student whose father had brought Shahram to Holmewood from Tehran, said Bairamian "was always looking for ways to change the school and make it better, and find the best in each pupil and help them develop."

Keenan says the latter tendency was one of Bairamian's great strengths—"finding out what you were interested in and giving you the tools." A second tendency, which became equally important for the Malek brothers as for other students, was the new headmaster's ferocity if you were caught wasting the opportunity. Keenan says that Bairamian would open the door to success, but any blessed boy risked "six of the best" if he didn't walk through it, and promptly. Still, Keenan adds, "We weren't scared of him. We all adored him. You couldn't help wanting him to like you."

Bairamian ran what another former student calls "a multicultural meritocracy," a notion that Keenan confirms, saying, "Holmewood was multicultural before the word was even invented." Bairamian's father, Sir Vahe Bairamian, had been recruited from Cyprus to be the chief judge in Sierra Leone and wound up an active recruiter for Holmewood, identifying and encouraging promising boys from successful families in West Africa. As Peter says, "I had never seen a black person before." But he found his best friends from among these African recruits, especially the Liberian Willmot Dennis and the Nigerian Robert Prest. They were athletic and whip-smart, and the Maleks both say they regret losing touch in the years that followed.

Keenan says the West African students were among the most popular—"cheerful, tough, great athletes. They were what everyone wanted to be." But for him, the Persian students also seemed fascinating, "these boys who in their spare time read squiggly books, back to front," no doubt a reference to the homework given by Mr. Bahar, the University of London student whom Amir had engaged to tutor the boys in Farsi. Keenan says racism was not just discouraged at Holmewood but also entirely unknown. In researching his film on the boys of Holmewood, he says everyone reported the same thing: even while there had been high-profile incidents of prejudice elsewhere in Britain, beginning with the late-1950s race riots in Notting Hill, when white working-class London "Teddy Boys" had set upon an expanding population of Caribbean immigrants, Holmewood seemed a world apart. "No one [at the school] experienced racism till secondary school. And then they were shocked to see it."

The school had one cultural bias: everyone took Bible study and only the Jewish boys were excused from going to chapel on Sundays. Bairamian and company were unconcerned that the Malek boys were Muslim-born—or that others in this multicultural community were not Christian. He still sent everyone for chapel, and, at the end of every morning assembly, he still recited his favourite verses from the Book of Revelation 21: 1–6. Keenan says the Scriptures were taught as parables, not as doctrine. And in the minds of the boys, "the only god was Bob."

The brothers agree, and say they heard the lessons more as literature than dogma, and they loved listening to Bairamian. This early, benign exposure seeded a life-long comfort with the observances and rituals of the Christian church, reinforcing their headmaster's teachings that all were equal.

The Maleks' recollections of their days at Holmewood make it sound like a rigorous, never-ending summer camp. The school was fiercely competitive: every two weeks, the teachers would review the boys' academic standings and then rearrange their desk assignments to acknowledge best to worst. There were 30 acres of grounds and, in Keenan's description, "one of the best cricket pitches in England." There was a broad stream running through stands of oak, beech, and silver birch, the perfect sylvan forest for boys playing pirates or Robin Hood—or for sneaking out and building midnight fires on which they would try to roast potatoes that they'd stolen in a "larder raid." There were the midnight swims and listening surreptitiously to pirate radio stations Radio Caroline and Radio Luxembourg on their mini transistor radios under the bed sheets after lights out.

Years later, when Peter and Shahram were writing their A Levels—the academic exams that are critical for getting into UK universities—they say it was the discipline and encouragement of Holmewood that made the difference.

"It was tough," Shahram says, "but good. I wouldn't change a bit of it. And I would do the same thing again." Decades later, he says, he'll be walking a trail on Vancouver's North Shore and catch the scent of a particular tree, and it will rush him back to "Scout Wood." Even the mundane and unromantic smell of fresh asphalt can whisk him back to a newly paved road through the forests of Kent.

And the boys thrived in the nurturing environment of Holmewood. The UK Eleven Plus exam, taken at the age of eleven, sets the stage for a student's future educational direction, and the teachings at Holmewood laid a solid groundwork for this important test.

Shahram won the History prize in 1962, which meant being included in a school trip to see David Lean's Academy Award–winning *Lawrence of Arabia* at the Metropole Cinema in London—certainly one of the most celebrated cultural events of the day. He also recalls fondly that his essay, titled "Sleep," was singled out, being published in the Holmewoodian school magazine of September 1963.

In the same year, Peter was one of only six students from Holmewood to win a scholarship in his preparatory school graduating year to Clayesmore School in Dorset. He subsequently decided to go to King's College Taunton, in Somerset. To Shahram, still at Holmewood for two more years, this seemed clear across the country, but the boys weathered the separation in good humour, both having found their footing and new sets of friends.

During school breaks and short holidays, the brothers were often entertained at the Wise home, enjoying the best tradition of English Christmas. Even in the early days, when they were deeply homesick and out of sorts, Shahram's main memories are of the warmth and kindness of the people, both in and out of school. In his first year away, Mrs. Wise came by the school one weekend day to take him to tea in Tunbridge Wells, and when she asked for the bill, the proprietor waved her off, saying, "It's free. I just love that little boy's eyes."

Mrs. Wise took the boys to pantomimes in London, including *Peter Pan*; to the Bertram Mills Circus, where they were enchanted by the acrobats, animals, and clowns; and to the cinema to watch Cliff Richard, the "English Elvis," and others—with stops in the Hamleys toy shop on Regent Street to see miniature trains and other toys the boys found "magical."

Through connections arranged by the Wises, the boys also spent school holidays with English families in Colchester, Essex, in the spring, where they learned to play table tennis, and in Poole, Dorset, for the 1963 Christmas holidays, where, upon receiving a gift from the family, Shahram reciprocated by giving them his beloved History prize. There was also a holiday at the warm home of a Mrs. Lloyd in Richmond upon Thames, where Shahram says they met exciting and slightly older non-boarding-school English teenagers, boys and girls who interacted freely, and who invited the Malek boys to dances and introduced them to the illicit dangers of teenage cigarette smoking.

In longer breaks and summer holidays, the boys fell into a happy rhythm of reuniting with family. In the first year, Amir and Mahin came to England for short visits, wanting to leave the boys lots of time to acclimatize before returning to Iran, even for a break. After that, however, Peter says, "We went to so many places." Amir loved to travel. He loved Germany, Mahin loved Paris, and everyone loved their summers in Iran. So, they spent school holidays travelling all around Europe, on beaches in the Mediterranean, in Spain or Italy or, on one particularly memorable trip, in Morocco. It was their first family foray into the African continent, and they were looking forward to a warm reprieve from the chill English winter. But even Holmewood House had better heating than Marrakesh or Casablanca. They shivered through the trip, marvelled at the raucous and exotic culture, grimaced at the odoriferousness of a particularly memorable cabbie—and then counted their blessings on a subsequent holiday to Tenerife in the Canary Islands.

The first family trip to America in 1963 began as a cruise on the SS France, a sparkling new passenger liner that, at 315 metres, was the longest passenger ship ever built. It sailed with 180 of France's best cooks, sauce and pastry chefs, rotisserie cooks, head waiters, and wine stewards, inspiring the *New York Times* food critic of the day, Craig Claiborne, to hail it as "the best French restaurant in the world." Peter and Shahram have a particularly fond recollection of eating steak for breakfast.

The Maleks boarded the ship in Le Havre and sailed to Southampton and then New York, waking up to see the Statue of Liberty outside their stateroom's porthole. After a short stay at the Bedford Hotel—including the pleasure of a steak that Peter was shocked to learn cost US$13 (at that time, half the cost of a new bicycle)—they flew to Miami, where they stayed at the Fontainebleau Miami Beach, the famed hotel where the James Bond movie *Goldfinger* was filmed around the same time. Then it was off to San Francisco, followed by a cozy drive down the Coast Road to Los Angeles, with seven immediate and extended family members tucked into a huge, red Chevy Impala convertible. The brothers remember motels, which seemed exotic in the day, and featured swimming pools, air-conditioned rooms, 24/7 television (at a time when UK TV ended every night at 11 p.m.) and, Peter's favourite, Cokes for 10 cents. Then they climbed aboard a Bonanza Airlines propeller plane to Las Vegas and a stay at the iconic Sands Hotel (scene of the original *Oceans 11*), before a short hop back to San Francisco and a long, long flight "home" to the UK.

Asked now to choose a favourite from all these trips, Mahin shrugs and says, "We were always very happy that we were all together." It's a response that reflects a family habit: the Maleks all seem to resist picking favourites—in all things—as if it might insult the other contenders, from grand buildings to holiday destinations.

Still, after the indulgences of international travel and the comforts and camaraderie of Holmewood, the next school, King's College Taunton, an all-boys school like Holmewood, was larger, older, more rigid, and at the time less multicultural—with the student body drawn mostly from the Somerset communities surrounding the grounds. Instead of Holmewood's one hundred students, with boarders distributed two or three to a room, King's had four hundred students, and the boys were bunked in vast dorms, in one case with thirty-six beds to a room lined up military style. The Maleks say that King's was a great school, but it was much less intimate at the time. They were unhappy to find no black students and, among a small minority, a flash of intolerance—although they both say none of the intercultural ribbing ever rose to the level of actual racism. Indeed, while Peter and Shahram fit right in, the local boys were more inclined to tease students from Wales. King's has progressed with the times into a fresh vigorous co-ed school, proud of the achievements of its many notable alumni, including the captain of England's cricket team!

Just as at Holmewood, the Maleks were expected to continue their Christian scholarship and observance, with daily services in the spartan and chilly 1908 King's Chapel. Shahram says, "We told them: 'But we're Muslims',", a complication that was immediately dismissed. Only the Jewish boys were exempt. In spite of the forced attendance, both Shahram and Peter say they enjoyed the cultural content and went on to comfortably pass their O Levels (UK high school accreditation) in Scripture. To this day, they feel totally at home in a Christian church.

The brothers made good friends at King's. Peter remained close with Richard Curtis, now a respected barrister, and Shahram best remembers Martin Trelawny of Felixstowe and David Porter from Poole, who introduced Shahram to Jimi Hendrix (the music, if regrettably not the man). Shahram also remembers being encouraged in table tennis by John Medley, a superb player, and the warmth and kindness of Ian Livingstone and John Clarke, the down-to-earth son of the local pastor.

They also fit in with the school's athletic scene. Peter was a valued member of the rugby team until he was kicked in the eye during a scrum. No one paid much attention until he was back in Iran on his next holiday and the family doctor diagnosed a detached retina, which Peter says was later repaired by "Mr. Greaves, a top surgeon on Harley Street in London." Peter says that Shahram enjoyed significant success as a long-distance runner.

Academically, though, after both the rigours and the flexibility of Holmewood, the boys were ready for anything once they arrived at King's. Under Mr. Bairamian's ambitious leadership, education at Holmewood had been classical but wide-ranging—lots of Latin, but very little memorization. Lacking a formal curriculum, each day's classes tended to reflect the current interests of the students and the current events of the time. As Keenan tells it, very few of the Holmewood faculty were formally trained, but Bairamian had an eye for natural ability. For example, John Bagnall showed up at the school intent upon selling encyclopedias, and hearing the passion of his pitch and the extent of his knowledge, Bairamian rejected the books, but hired the man. Bagnall immediately took over as Oak housemaster, a role that had been Bairamian's, and enjoyed a long career as a popular leader and an excellent English teacher. On the latter, Shahram recalls that Bagnall always smoked a sweet-smelling pipe, and on one occasion when he had briefly stepped out of the classroom, Shahram went over to his table by the blackboard, picked up a piece of tobacco out of the round tin, and put it in his mouth, only to discover a bitter taste much different from the chocolaty smell!

Against this casual standard, King's College seemed more orthodox and less flexible, although both boys were impressed by the standard of the language instruction and both say that Mr. Edwards, the math teacher, was top-notch. With that preparation—and standing on the firm foundation of the Holmewood experience—Peter left King's with 3 A Levels with marks that were sufficient to win entry to the civil engineering program at the University of Edinburgh, the best university in Scotland and consistently one of the top 10 in the United Kingdom.

The choice of degree felt preordained. Amir Malek was a civil engineer, and when the children were small, he delighted in taking them to job sites. Peter says, "He was my role model." Shahram, on the other hand, was worried about his marks and the scientific rigour necessary to master the engineering program. But after visiting Peter for the first time, he had his heart set on following his brother once again. "Edinburgh is so beautiful. It's like a fairy-tale city," he says. He left King's College at the age of seventeen and enrolled in the Basil Paterson Tutorial College, also in Edinburgh. In the UK system, Basil Paterson is commonly known as "a crammer," a small, independent college that specializes in preparing students to write their A Levels. While there, his parents had heard about Dr. Reza Sabri-Tabrizi, a senior lecturer in the Department of Persian Studies at the university who had obtained his doctorate on the life of the English poet William Blake. They asked Dr. Tabrizi to take Shahram under his wing.

Shahram assumed that his next challenge was going to be convincing his father that he was not going to study engineering. But Amir said, "Don't worry, business and economics are very good subjects to study," and the next year, Shahram, too, was accepted at Edinburgh University to study economics and social sciences. He credits Dr. Tabrizi with being generous during that important year and afterwards, helping him learn Persian literature and spirituality, and taking him to the University Staff Club on Chambers Street for lunches and dinners, a big honour for a seventeen-year-old. "He was a true mentor," says Shahram, "and played a big role in my getting accepted by Edinburgh."

This is one of those times in life when a previously orderly existence can come badly off the rails, a time when, after eight years in a boarding-school setting with their every move monitored and regi-mented, two young students are suddenly completely on their own. As Peter says, "A lot of people lose themselves, drinking and party-ing." But the brothers remained focused, conscious always of their parents' support and concern. They were more disappointed than resentful when Amir refused to buy them a car, partly on the basis that he considered it risky to put his young sons at the wheel of a car.

He was proved right. One evening, the brothers were invited by an older friend on an outing to a pub in Howgate, south of the city. They joined a party of seven, crowded into an aging Austin sedan. The broth-ers are circumspect about what followed, saying only that on the way home from the pub, Shahram was sitting in the front seat, while Peter was among those stuffed into the back. The crash that followed was gruesome enough that the Scotsman newspaper ran a large photo of their battered vehicle. Stuffed among fellow students in the back seat, Peter escaped largely unscathed, but Shahram, who was in the front, smashed his face against the dashboard and badly broke his jaw. He required thirty-nine stitches to close up gashes over his nose and eye. He still has a sharp, deep scar on the bridge of his nose from that accident.

Ever on the lookout for a bright side, Shahram says, "The young nurses were very kind," and as luck would have it, the surgeon on call was a leading professor at the Edinburgh University Medical School. Mother Mahin was beside herself with concern, but by the time she got to see her battered son, she had turned philosophical, arguing against corrective plastic surgery on the basis that scars give men character.

Shahram used the situation to his advantage. "When someone else drives, this is what happens," he told his father. It worked. Amir bought them a new red Ford Capri with a black vinyl top, hoping that the modern technology and the direct responsibility would keep the boys safe in their future adventures.

After the restrained English years, they loved the Scottish people, who they found relaxed and easygoing. Though the brothers were surprised to find different sorts of cultural intolerance. The Scots were perfectly happy to welcome them as fellow students, whatever their national heritage. But when they heard them speak in the plum tones acquired through years of English public-school tutelage, they said, "The first thing you need to do is get rid of that [English] accent!"

The brothers made lifelong friends at university, including one of Peter's fellow engineering students, an Egyptian-Lebanese named Mohammed Hamza. They also befriended older Iranian students who were in Edinburgh pursuing post-graduate degrees, including Fred Adab, an architect and intellectual who was working on a graduate degree in planning and who later helped the family during the revolutionary period, and Mozaffar Rostampour, a PhD engineering student who they remember as always kind and impeccably polite. There was also Saleem Khan, a warm and generous undergraduate in the architecture department, and Touraj Besharat, another undergraduate student, and his congenial Scottish wife, Sheila; all were gracious and had a worldly outlook. (All these friends, save Saleem Khan who is in London, have since migrated to Canada as well, with both Fred, Mozaffar, Touraj, and Sheila coming to Vancouver.) Although the boys were inclined to look for a line between being worldly and being political, Shahram recalls Fred decrying the Shah as being out of touch with his people. When Fred said, "The Shah must go," Shahram asked, "But why? And who will replace him?" It was an optimistic time, and Fred, at least, was confident that such optimism was justified. Iran, he said, was a civilized, cultured, and well-advanced country with a population that was up to the challenge of managing its affairs without a king or a dictator at the helm. It's a conversation that would reverberate in later years.

The Maleks found Scotland to be beautiful, yet different from England. The people were generous and down-to-earth. And Edinburgh's architecture is magnificent, nature coexists with formality on Princes Street and throughout the elegant streets and parks of New Town, while Arthur's Seat, an ancient volcano, stands majestically within a mile of the famous castle.

The university is part of this heritage, dating back to 1583. The undergraduate students were primarily from Scottish and English schools, and it was a rewarding and pleasant environment, especially for two boys accustomed to an English boarding school. They were thrilled that you could go out with girls and, at the age of eighteen, drop into a pub and order a whisky just like in the movies!

Looking back wistfully on that era, and more generally on the time, Shahram says: "We were lucky enough. We had freedom, and we used it well. It was one of the best times in my life."

This period also featured one of the brothers' favourite holidays. In 1968, Amir decided that the whole family would fly around the world in sixteen days. Starting in London, the brothers flew Pan American to Tehran for a short visit with extended family and a rendezvous with their parents. Then, after stopovers in Delhi and Bangkok, where they remember being served tropical fruit in the airport, they went on to Hong Kong for four days, with a side trip to Macao. Next was a four-day stop in Japan. Landing in Tokyo, they took a bullet train south to Kyoto, where they stayed in a traditional guesthouse. Then it was off to Honolulu, where Shahram remembers the locals exclaiming—positively, this time—over the cultured English accent that had rankled his Scottish schoolmates. The final stop was in San Francisco for a visit with a favourite cousin and then back to London.

The brothers describe the whole trip in the breathless pace that it clearly must have occurred. They marvelled at a world of opportunity and revelled in their chance to fly through these disparate capitals and cultures. And while it took some time later to fully recognize or appreciate it, they luxuriated in a world (notwithstanding the Cold War) that seemed overwhelmingly at peace.

EVOLUTION-REVOLUTION

The news in the past few decades has been awash with stories of refugees from Iran, Iraq, Afghanistan, Lebanon, Syria, North Africa, and Central America. These are people who, in fear and desperation, have flown from danger, conscious that they are leaving a country, a landscape—a home—that they may never see again, and who are longing for that place.

But there is a perverse alternative awaiting the lucky young Malek men who, after a buttoned-down upbringing, have been loosed on the world. During the days in Scotland, Peter and Shahram had emerged from the tight strictures of an English boys' school into the freedom and independence of burgeoning adulthood, and now—it seemed suddenly—they were facing graduation and the imminent prospect that they would *have* to go home again. It's not that home held no appeal. It's just that life in Edinburgh—and London—was the greater temptation. Peter says, "We were having such a good time." As he approached his own graduation in 1971, he phoned home to say that he was thinking of doing a master's or maybe a PhD. "My dad said, 'Why?' And I didn't really have a good reason."

Knowing that Peter eventually wanted to join the family business, Amir arranged for him to spend a transitional year in France, interning with a series of prominent international firms that had partnered with Armeh on big projects in and around Tehran. He worked with Sif Bachy, an engineering and design firm that was doing major foundation and tunnel-boring work for the extension to the Paris Metro, and with L'Entreprise Jean Lefebvre, one of the oldest and largest road- and bridge-building firms in France—one of many connections that would prove important in the years to come. Renting a studio apartment in the 8th arrondissement, steps from the Champs-Élysées, and driving a new, orange BMW 2002, Peter soon found that he could have "such a good time" in Paris as well as in Edinburgh. He also enjoyed what he later began to think of as his first experience in constructional espionage: he got a chance to work with great people at the leading edge of innovation in his field, and they paid him, even as he was learning lessons that would serve him directly in his work. It was a new and different kind of education.

At the end of the year, he drove that Bimmer to Tehran, accompanied for most of the trip by Pirouz, the husband of a cousin. They made the most of the adventure at every stage, winding their way through Italy, down the Adriatic, and stopping in Greece to visit new-found friends, brother and sister Yannis and Sofia Aronis, who Peter had met in Paris. Then, they continued on to Turkey, lapping up the extraordinary scenery along the Black Sea, but resolving not to share some of the details of the trip with Mahin. (The region was peaceful, but there were still some treacherous roads, and some parts of the country where you wouldn't stop if you didn't have to.) One of the most memorable aspects of the trip was the transition from "the bad roads in Turkey" to Iran, "which was almost like going back into Europe." Once he hit the wide, smooth pavement in his own relatively wealthy country, he put foot to floor and drove the twelve hours from the Turkish border in one hurried day, only to have the BMW break down just inside the city limits in Tehran. Mahmoud Agha, the long-standing and loyal family driver and major-domo, turned out for a late-night rescue, and the homecoming Peter had been putting off became, instead, a sweet culmination.

Amir didn't give Peter much time to settle in. "As soon as I arrived, my father put me to work." Armeh had just completed the 105,000-seat Aryamehr Stadium and a colossal, man-made lake. The stadium was the first part of a sports complex that Armeh was building in time for the 1974 Asian Games and the company was soon tapped to add a sports hall, an indoor swimming pool, a velodrome, and other buildings, all built to Olympic specifications to accommodate a long-term plan for Tehran to compete as the location for the 1984 Olympic Games. Peter started as an assistant superintendent, overseeing construction of a 12,000-seat ice-sports arena and then, as well, a sports hall for basketball and other indoor sports.

Shahram, meanwhile, had been enjoying his own good time in Edinburgh, followed, after graduation, by a summer spent in the family apartment in the tony London neighbourhood of St. John's Wood off Finchley Road. He, too, was stalling, trying to come up with credible reasons to stay in the UK. But he read about an MBA program at the new Iran Centre for Management Studies (ICMS) in Tehran, the brainchild of the industrialist and Harvard scholar Dr. Habib Ladjevardi. The program was based on the Harvard MBA and delivered by faculty on leave from Harvard University. Before moving to London, Shahram had taken a side trip from Edinburgh to Glasgow to write the GMAT (Graduate Management Admissions Test), on which, he claims, "I did horribly." So, he was surprised to be offered a position in the second ICMS MBA class, saying, with impractical modesty, that in a group heavily dominated by top local and international students, "I think I was a diversity hire"—a twenty-two-year-old British boarding school and UK university applicant amid a class of brilliant students whose average age was in the mid-thirties. Shahram's self-effacing self-assessment notwithstanding, Professor E. Robert Livernash, head of the Harvard faculty, remarked during that year that the ICMS class was superior to the Harvard classes in the same year, a testament to the calibre of students, for many of whom English was a second language.

Regardless of the acceptance, Shahram was holding out, still loving life in London. So, Amir—the more seasoned negotiator—invited Shahram to meet him at the family apartment in Nice. There, Shahram says, his father, who had flown to Nice from Tehran just for this meeting, was "very patient." Amir said, "I really want you to come back to Iran." And Shahram said he really didn't want to go. The ICMS experience looked like a return to boarding school—for practical purposes, it *was* a return to boarding school: the students were all going to be bunking together, pounding through a one-year version of the two-year Harvard MBA. Every time Amir made a plea, Shahram offered an argument. For example, he complained that he had left London with nothing but the clothes in a single suitcase and the Ford Capri was still parked, casually, on the street in St. John's Wood. Amir, no quitter, called a friend in London and said he could keep the car if he promised to move it. And, although Shahram says, "I had tears in my eyes," by the end of the fourth day, they boarded a flight together back to Tehran.

THERE FOLLOWED, FOR both sons, an apprenticeship very like the one that Amir had served himself.

In his autobiography, Amir Malek writes that he was the scion of a respected and successful family from the central Iranian city of Yazd. (Yazdān is the Persian word for god, and yazdī is a common suffix identifying the bearer as a native or inhabitant of Yazd.) Amir's grandfather, Agha Koochak, was a prosperous and upstanding merchant with a strong sense of integrity and a streak of stubborn determination. In the mid-1800s, Agha Koochak was under increasing pressure from the extortionist governor of Yazd to pay a large political graft, for no purpose other than to enrich the governor. Agha Koochak resisted this injustice until it became clear that his life might be in danger, at which point he set out on the 600-kilometre journey to Tehran to make his case before the Shah. Somewhat to his surprise, he won an audience—and the argument. The Shah ultimately replaced the governor and honoured Agha Koochak with the title Malek-ol-Tojjar, Lord Merchant of Yazd.

The Lord Merchant's offspring were also successful, but Amir's father died from a heart attack at age fifty-two, when Amir, the youngest of eight children, was only two years old. Not long after, Amir's mother, Roghieh, moved to Tehran, encouraged by her second-eldest son Akbar to bring her two youngest children (the only two still living at home) to the capital, where they might get a better education.

Akbar soon moved to Germany, and in 1937, he paid for his little brother to join him in Berlin. Amir, then just sixteen, took a circuitous train trip from Iran through Russia and eastern Europe to take up an apprenticeship in masonry and carpentry and, later, to enrol in the Berlin Polytechnic University in Charlottenburg, to study engineering.

Amir passed much of this period largely insulated from the dangers and privations of the war, although food rationing was part of everyday life. He worked for the huge German construction conglomerate Philipp Holzmann, sharpening his skills even as he was upgrading his credentials. He told family in later years that he was constantly aware of the conflict—his ability to travel was restricted as it was for the German population, and he lost friends and a teacher who were sent to the front and didn't return—but living in a wartime capital, getting news only from a government-controlled media, he had no real sense of all that was going on.

Shortly after graduating in 1944, when the war itself was beginning to close in on Berlin, Akbar was able to intervene again, helping Amir to move to Switzerland, where he worked for another large construction company, Conradin Zschokke, on a large bridge over the Rhone River in Geneva.

When the war ended in 1945, he made his way to Paris, beginning a lifelong love affair with that city, and then quickly to Marseille, where he boarded a Turkish freighter for the trip back to Iran. He took up employment with the Independent Institute of Hydro, a Ministry of Agriculture agency that was independent in name only. With verve and enthusiasm, he threw himself into his work, only to find that his efforts were completely ignored, at which point—telegraphing a familial impatience with government—he resigned in less than a year.

Even before setting out on his own, however, Amir had been moonlighting as a translator, which afforded him the financial independence not just to quit his government sinecure but also to begin a speculative and surprisingly ambitious construction project for distant relatives from Yazd who were setting up an automobile dealership in Tehran.

His first independent undertaking was a complicated 1,600-square-metre reinforced-concrete building with a large interior showroom. At a time when concrete was still being mixed by hand

and there were no facilities in Iran for testing and controlling the quality of construction materials, an older, more conservative contractor might have urged his client to settle for a simpler structure, with smaller spaces, or at least a set of pillars to hold the weight of the open span. But leveraging the skills he had acquired in Europe and the creativity that would mark his construction career for decades to come, Amir tackled the job successfully, winning praise for what was regarded as daring and finely executed work.

Word got around. Even while Amir was still completing his first project, a budding admirer invited him to bid on a contract to dig the foundation for a large maternity hospital that was to be built by the Society for the Protection of Mothers and Newborns. Amir won the bid, and even before his new crew finished the excavation, he won the contract for the construction work as well and, with a partner, formed the Armeh Construction Company (armé is the French word for reinforced—béton armé being "reinforced concrete"). The job was complicated and political, featuring labour challenges and interference from above—which is also a consistent theme in the development world—and Amir wound up buying out his partner before the 8,000-square-metre project was completed.

While this work was in progress, Amir was recruited to bid on the new, 3,000-square-metre laboratory for the Pasteur Institute, the French non-profit medical organization. This was yet another project that demanded the kind of exacting standards that Amir had adopted in his early apprenticeships with the leading German construction firms, as well as the innovative brilliance that would continue to mark his career. Again, his bid succeeded and, again, the work won accolades and yet more attention.

Google Amir Malekyazdi (in Persian, Malek from Yazd) today and you'll see evidence of the success that followed. Through the ensuing decades, Armeh tackled a series of increasingly complicated public and private projects, including airports, roads, bridges, tunnels, railways, warehouses, and schools. Armeh would frequently be the low bidder, finding ways, through clever engineering and good management, to deliver on time and on budget. Armeh also earned a reputation as the company that could come in and bat cleanup if another contractor had taken on something complicated and failed. On highway projects, especially, which could involve challenging locations, bridges, tunnels, swamps, or high ledges, Armeh would get the call to come to the rescue—but only if it were prepared to complete the work for the same payment agreed upon by the original contractor. In his biography, Amir writes, "We knew from experience that haggling on this subject was useless." But he also says, "I won't deny that I also relished the challenge of completing a project deemed impossible by a competitor."

Two other important trends emerged during this long run of successes. First, Armeh made a large number of contacts among some of Europe's most ambitious and innovative design, engineering, and construction firms. Large projects often required the collaboration of consulting engineers or the importation of new practices, most easily accessed through these international partnerships. Armeh learned to look for the best help in Europe, and those European leaders learned that, when they were working in Iran, Armeh was the best.

The other trend was less helpful. As public sector jobs got bigger and more complex, Amir encountered an increasing amount of government interference and game-playing. He had never engaged in politics and was determined always to succeed on the quality of his work, not on lobbying or corruption. In his autobiography, he wrote of a particularly troublesome contract for the Iranian Air Force: "My contempt for the usual games played in such instances provided me with the feeling I had the moral upper hand, and I drew my courage and strength from a spiritual source far above any temporal threat of a menacing authority." It was an armour destined to be tested beyond its limits.

By 1969, the company that Amir had started as a brash twenty-something was the toast of Tehran. "Government agencies had come to recognize Armeh as the only company that could implement the tough projects too daunting for other construction firms to tackle," Amir wrote. So, it was inconvenient when Armeh came in as high bidder on the Aryamehr Stadium and artificial lake. It was just the kind of project he had come to enjoy—complex, high-profile, and with an extra-tight timeframe because the government wanted the stadium in place for a 1971 celebration of 2,500 years of the Persian empire. So, he was disappointed to be priced out of the competition, even if he might not have been surprised to lose the bid, whether due to price or to politics. Fred Adab, the brothers' university friend, who is now a Vancouver architect, said it was widely known in Tehran at the time that many major government projects were awarded on the basis of the bidder's political connections. And while Armeh had come to the rescue on many large projects and had built a reputation for excellence, honesty, independence, and what Adab calls "Mr. Malek's genius," the company was not on the list of political favourites.

In that light, Amir was confused when he got a call only weeks later from Gholam Reza Nikpay, the Tehran liaison for Skidmore, Owings & Merrill, the giant US engineering firm that had been put in charge of architectural design and supervision of the project. Writing about the episode in his autobiography, Amir said that Nikpay (who would go on to become the mayor of Tehran) laid out the challenge in the most unsentimental terms. He said that the deadline for completing the stadium was less than eighteen months away, leaving just fifteen months for the actual work, given the inevitable start-up delays. Yet the government had already sent invitations to prominent guests—mostly monarchs and heads of state—to attend the celebrations less than two years hence. It would be embarrassing—for the whole country—if the stadium wasn't ready, Nikpay told him.

When Amir asked what he could do to help, Nikpay said he had raised the matter with members of the Iranian Cabinet, who agreed that Armeh was the only Iranian company likely to complete the job by the required date—and with that, he invited Amir to take on the project after all.

It was flattering, of course, but Amir was not the sort to elbow successful bidders out of the way to satisfy someone in government, and he said so. He soon learned, however, that the other bidders—who had been summoned and were actually waiting in the next room—had been convinced to withdraw. All that remained was for Amir to accept the work and, in keeping with what had become tradition, to accept the price set by the lowest bidder. Amir writes: "I shook hands on the deal, so enamored with undertaking such a prestigious project and accepting such a colossal responsibility that I refrained from taking any measures that could secure us a higher profit."

This might be read as the kind of ambition—perhaps a combination of pride and bravado or maybe just a commitment to a public good—that would rise again in the hearts of his sons. Amir had done the math and estimated a higher cost than was afforded in the contract. But he had come into unfinished projects on countless occasions and found a way not just to complete others' underbid work but also to do it at a profit. He seemed ever confident that he would find a way—and the record showed that he frequently succeeded.

This, however, would not be the end of the political and bureaucratic interference in the the Aryamehr Stadium. For example, while one arm of government was demanding an impossible work schedule, another arm was prohibiting the import of crucial building materials. But Armeh met the deadline. It even finished the lake, which required excavating a huge basin from a particularly porous base of limestone and sand, creating a unique, diluted asphalt to make the basin watertight, and then manufacturing innovative new rollers that could apply and secure pavement up the lake's steep banks.

It took a month to fill the lake using water drawn from the Karaj River and from wells dug deep around the stadium. And it took Armeh more than four years to get fully paid. It duelled with government officials who used every imaginable excuse to argue that the work was somehow lacking and that Armeh didn't deserve its cheque. But a sufficient number of independent observers ultimately sided with Armeh, Amir got paid for his efforts, and the stadium still stands today, robust and beautiful. The revolutionary government of Iran removed the original honorific Aryamehr—or "Light of the Aryans"—one of many titles that had been bestowed upon the overthrown Mohammad Reza Shah Pahlavi, and renamed it Azadi, but the building remains in use today.

Still, by the time Amir won the argument and received fair payment, he was thoroughly soured on public works. "After our challenges in constructing the 105,000-seat stadium, instead of being congratulated and rewarded, we were punished ... As a result, I made up my mind to expand our involvement within the private sector, and to steer clear of future government dealings."

THIS WAS THE Tehran to which Peter and Shahram returned in the early 1970s. Their father was prosperous and widely admired within Iran and among many top-flight construction, architecture, and engineering companies in Europe and North America. The brothers were eventually given their own capacious offices in Armeh's Tehran headquarters, which were housed in what had been a half-finished luxury hotel on Vesal-e Shirazi Avenue that Amir had taken over and converted into a gleaming office building, even dredging under the building's finished structure to add two levels of underground parking. Peter and Shahram each had a full-time secretary (while today they share both their office space and their assistant). The whole family lived in a large and beautiful hilltop home, replete with pool and tennis court, which the locals sometimes referred to as "The White House" even though it was actually pink, Mahin's favourite colour. And they had holiday homes in Nice, Paris, London, and, their favourite, a thickly forested 25-acre waterfront estate on the Caspian Sea that had a winding driveway leading to a hilltop villa designed by the Iranian-Armenian architect Babaian. On the water side, it also boasted a large formal garden, a tennis court, and a beach house with a daytime kitchen and a big veranda. It's where they spent the best part of every summer—and where they imagined spending innumerable summers to come.

Tehran was a safe, prosperous, and open society at this time. Peter remembers that there were "fantastic restaurants and really good clubs." Discos were all the rage. "Iran," Peter says, "had become a very Western country." The previous king, Reza Shah, who reigned from 1925 to 1941, had done much to modernize the society, as well as the economy, banning the veil and working toward the emancipation of women. When his son and successor, Mohammad Reza Pahlavi, came to power in 1941, he followed a similar path. A devout Shia Muslim, the younger Shah nevertheless maintained a tolerance for other religions—Baha'is, Orthodox Christians, Jews, and minority Sunni Muslims. Shahram says, "As long as you were apolitical, it was fine." And the Maleks were—and remain—resolutely apolitical. Amir and Armeh had done some of their best work on large public projects without ever taking a position *with* government or *against* the people. They took pride in their work and, compared to some of the more prominent players in the highest government circles, were modest in their habits and comportment.

In 1974, Amir began edging away from government work, refocusing his energies on a large property he had purchased decades earlier in the tony Vanak district of northern Tehran. It was 2.2 hectares, and soon after he bought it, he laid out the roads, registered individual construction sites, built a large central lagoon, and planted trees over the whole property. In the time since, Amir wrote in his autobiography, "The trees had grown tall and the land had transformed into a charming and lush environment." So, he set about planning a 1-million-square-foot multi-use development that he called Parc des Princes, a name chosen by Mahin because of her love of France. It featured three high-rises of 16, 21, and 25 storeys and a shopping centre, and became the largest private-sector project in Iran at the time. Amir hired the Italian architects Barsanti and the legendary Vico Magistretti from Milan; the structural engineer Corielli; and French control engineers Socotec to provide an additional layer of control for the structural design, delighted to think the result would be a showpiece in the Armeh portfolio. He also gave Peter significant responsibility for project management.

Even before Parc des Princes was far into construction, Armeh was offered a second property, similar in size and just half a kilometre away. Here, the company worked with the iconic Iranian architect Abdol-Aziz Farmanfarmaian, who had been joint architect with Skidmore, Owings & Merrill of Chicago on the Asian Games complex. The new development, Vanak Park, named after the prime north Tehran neighbourhood, comprised four 24-storey luxury condominium buildings, a massive club house, a shopping centre, four tennis courts, two heated swimming pools, and a children's play area, again over a million square feet in total building area. So, Peter moved to take the lead on Vanak Park, while Shahram stepped into a slightly more junior role at Parc des Princes.

They were heady days. While neither brother is temperamentally flashy, and both understood the benefit of keeping a relatively low profile, they both used their first big cheques to buy nice cars. Peter bought a white Mercedes SLC 2+2 coupe—the conservative marque of choice at the time—and Shahram, after pleading with his father and winning over his mother as an ally, a burgundy Jaguar sedan. At work, they revelled in the challenges of the projects and the responsibility they had been given by their father.

In a new financial model that was just emerging across many markets, Armeh raised money for construction by pre-selling individual apartments. Sales were good since there was a ready market of people wanting to downsize from larger homes, and in this respect, too, Tehran seemed to be ahead of its time. Unfortunately, on a site visit midway through construction on Parc des Princes, Amir spotted what he felt was an inadequate bundle of reinforcing steel and he questioned the structural specifications in the buildings, which were supposed to meet California earthquake standards. A professional peer review confirmed his concern—the design was critically flawed. The vaunted French engineering firm Socotec had glossed over the drawings and left Armeh with an enormously expensive dilemma: accept a standard that was common in Tehran, but potentially unsafe in a region that is known to be prone to earthquakes, or start tearing out interior features to allow for a structural strengthening of all three buildings. The brothers were amazed by their father's composure, and remain proud of his conscientious response. The reinforcement was going to be incredibly expensive and would impose long delays.

And they knew from the standards common among other projects that, even by current design parameters, the existing building would be no worse than some relatively new buildings already standing. But Amir was unhesitating. He demanded that the French engineering firm replace its consultants, and he sacked the general manager of the project company, replacing him with Shahram. When Armeh's chief engineer, Fred Hovsepian, a no-nonsense American-educated bear of a man, challenged Shahram's promotion as premature, saying that Amir's younger son was "too young and too mild," Amir responded with the same confident certainty, telling Shahram, "If you have any problems, you just ask me."

The massive reinforcement effort delayed the project by almost two years, and it outraged some condo purchasers. It also dampened Shahram's newly gained business confidence. He says, "My whole world was a nightmare. I couldn't sleep at night." Yet, "Our father never complained. He was just very calm and matter of fact about the whole thing, setting his mind to do the task at hand even though he must have been aware of the potential disaster of reinforcing and rebuilding a virtually completed million-square-foot residential and commercial complex." The European consultants conceded that no remedial work of this scale had ever been done in Europe or elsewhere.

Everyone—and no one—anticipated what came next. In the middle 1970s, Iran seemed a pillar of stability in the Middle East. It was prosperous—the second-largest exporter of oil in the world—and peaceful, a US ally that was safely distanced from the ongoing conflicts between the Arab world and Israel. Some Iranians complained of government corruption, and in a society that prided itself on being a meritocracy, people resented the oil wealth that seemed to be flowing unfairly to a well-connected elite. But even while protests mounted in the streets, few observers seriously thought the Shah's regime to be in danger. Indeed, in his 1982 book, *Keeping the Faith: Memoirs of a President*, Jimmy Carter wrote that as late as June 1978, the CIA was advising that Iran "is not in a revolutionary or even a pre-revolutionary situation."

Throughout the autumn of 1978, however, protests increased in size and violence. By early December, thousands of Iranians were taking to the streets, denouncing the Shah as autocratic and decrying his continuing close relationship with the United States. And, in the international media, an increasing amount of attention was focused on the Ayatollah Ruhollah Khomeini, a radical cleric who had been banished from Iran in 1964 for his anti-government activism and who, by the late 1970s, had taken up residence in Paris. Khomeini was emerging as the heir-apparent should the Shah abandon his position or be overthrown.

Amid this turmoil, the Malek family went out of their way to take no notice whatsoever. Amir later wrote: "I was certain that the Revolution was only at war with the corrupt practices of the established system, and that it would not in any way interfere with ongoing development programs unless they were deemed useless or extravagant. As a consequence of this well-meaning assessment of the political atmosphere, even in the heat of street demonstrations, strikes and detentions, Armeh's road paving equipment was employed in the capital's chaotic avenues, trying to keep pace with our exacting schedule." Amir and his sons stayed out of the conversation and continued their work. Even after revolutionary forces broke open the armories in the breached military barracks and allowed people to seize and distribute weapons, which they then fired in the streets indiscriminately, Armeh continued to engage its workforce, making its payroll and meeting its one-floor-per-week construction target on Parc des Princes, even when that meant pouring concrete against the background of resounding gunfire.

Notwithstanding Amir's courage, his determination—his apparent conviction that, if he just did the right thing and stayed out of the politics, things would turn out—his bankers were less optimistic. Spooked by the increasing chaos leading up to the Revolution, Armeh's financiers in Iran and Europe decided the risk was too great and they cut off project funding for Parc des Princes and Vanak Park, even refusing to deliver on a line of credit that had just been approved by the Dutch bank ABN. Worse, they did so at a time when Amir had taken Mahin for an off-season pilgrimage to Mecca, in Saudi Arabia, and a large payment to contractors and almost two thousand workers was coming due at Parc des Princes. Upon hearing this, Amir calmly instructed Shahram to go and see Dara Vahabzadeh, the scion of a respected business family and president of the Bank of Iran and Holland. Given the bank's long history with Armeh, Amir felt there was a good chance they could secure an emergency line of credit. After making his way through the military Jeeps and trucks parked outside the bank's head office in downtown Tehran and being ushered into the president's private office, Shahram introduced himself and made the request. Shahram says now that he still remembers Vahabzadeh's exact words, as he hurriedly packed up his office contents to leave, probably for good, "Are you being serious? The country is falling apart and you are asking me for money!" Shahram left empty-handed, just two days before payment was due to Parc des Princes workers and contractors.

Alone at the Parc des Princes project office, a despondent Shahram took a call from Ms. Poshtiban, Amir's executive assistant of many years, who asked Shahram to confirm a meeting the following day with the company's lawyer, the long-time family advisor Ali Shahidzadeh. Amir had set up these private weekly meetings so his sons could discuss project-related legal issues and learn about Iranian law. On the verge of cancelling this session, which seemed pointless in the moment, Shahram had a change of heart and confirmed the appointment. It's well that he did. On hearing about the Parc des Princes financial issue, Shahidzadeh, then in his eighties, said simply: "Meet me tomorrow morning at seven-thirty at the Bank of Tehran." Shahram was still unsure what to expect when he arrived at the bank and was led into a second-floor boardroom. There, even as protesters were setting buses afire outside on Shah Reza Avenue, Shahidzadeh opened a Samsonite briefcase to reveal an amount, in cash, equal to US$300,000—a lot of money today, but an extraordinary amount in 1978. It was sufficient to meet the Parc des Princes payroll. Again, the details remain sharp in Shahram's memory. He said that Shahidzadeh simply said, "This is yours." And when Shahram asked if he needed a receipt, Shahidzadeh replied, "No, this is a loan to you, and I expect you, personally, to repay it."

Looking back, Shahram says he is still touched both by the generosity of the gesture, and by Shahidzadeh's absolute trust. This magnanimity was far from the general image people had of Shahidzadeh. "He had a reputation for being very frugal," Shahram says. "He wore the same-style simple suit every day. He worked in an office building with no elevator." Yet he would freely hand nearly a third of a million dollars to a twenty-something with full—and ultimately well-justified—confidence that it would be repaid in kind. To put it in perspective, that money was equivalent to the price of one of the Malek family's earlier homes in North Tehran, a modern classic that Abdol-Aziz Farmanfarmaian had designed at Amir's behest in 1960. In fact, Amir ultimately sold it specifically to make good on the Shahidzadeh debt.

The story illustrates the degree to which the Maleks and their close associates believed that they still had a future in Tehran. It was their home, and until now, the stable base for a range of construction and development ventures that had earned the family both prosperity and an excellent reputation. They were in no hurry to sacrifice either, despite a political situation that they saw as transitional—not fully unravelling. But even as the Maleks continued to do their work and meet their commitments, they couldn't fully insulate themselves from the unfolding crisis. They were at increasing risk precisely because they were among the few developers and contractors still working and still paying their bills. Gangs of previously unseen "labourers" began showing up, claiming that they had not been paid and demanding satisfaction—in cash and immediately.

On January 17, 1979, the protestors got their wish. Mohammad Reza Pahlavi, the last Shah of Iran, boarded a plane to Egypt. Two weeks later Khomeini returned from Paris, dismissed the transitional government, and installed a revolutionary council under a religious-nationalist opposition leader named Mehdi Bazargan.

In the stressful days that followed, Amir tells a story that exemplifies the conditions that prevailed under this new, unsteady regime. "Armeh's headquarters were occupied by a large horde demanding that the company pay money that it 'owed' to workers as soon as possible. Many of these hostage takers were strangers, opportunists who had never had anything to do with the Armeh Company. Included in the crowd were also a few Armeh employees who had been on the company payroll. According to our accounting records, these workers had been paid their wages and were not owed a penny." But, Amir went on, "my error was that I heeded the advice of the Ministry of Labour, and in order to put an end to the conflict, I paid a large sum of cash to the crowd of bogus creditors. I mistakenly thought that by doing so, I could appease the mob and that the turmoil would come to an end. This, of course, did not happen. As a rule, when one tries to

cater to the unjust demands of a group of freeloaders and extortion-
ists, the problem snowballs."

Armeh persevered over the warnings of friends and business
colleagues alike, only to have another mob show up, once again
demanding cash payouts.

Things got even more tense when another impromptu sit-in at
the Armeh head office triggered a visit from the now-revolution-
ary Ministry of Labour. These were not your usual bureaucrats and
inspectors. Known as the *siajamegan*—the "Black Clad"—they were
enforcers, mostly young men with the swagger and threatening atti-
tude that seems almost inevitable when you're all armed with Uzi
submachine guns. The *siajamegan* leader, however, a middle-aged
man named Haji Lotfi, set about questioning both sides and quickly
established that the troublemakers were just that: they weren't employees or contractors, they were just people trying to extort money. Lotfi
chased them off and then followed up the next day by helping the
Maleks to collect a debt of their own—an overdue payment owed to
Armeh by a government department. Bijan, one of Haji Lotfi's lieu-
tenants, asked Shahram to drive him in the company BMW to the
government office in question, on Takhte-Jamshid Avenue. Upon
entering the high-rise office building, he asked Shahram to wait in the
lobby, drew his Colt revolver, and entered the elevator. He came back
twenty minutes later with the cheque made out to Armeh. Ever happy
to have his default to optimism confirmed, Shahram says, "They were
kind of nice people. And since we were young and wore jeans, we
didn't fit their image of the *ancien régime* greedy businessperson!"

After the Shah left the country in February 1979, a host of competing militias had emerged, all jockeying for power—or merely for
revolutionary plunder. On March 20, 1979, Peter and Shahram were at
home with Amir while their mother and sisters were away on a trip to

Paris. Shahram and Amir were both already asleep when the dog, a male collie named Lassie, began barking a warning. When Peter looked out from his bedroom window, he saw ten or fifteen armed militia members trying to force open one of the big iron gates at the front driveway. They were shouting, demanding entry, and when only the dog answered, Peter says, they sprayed the front of the house with machine gun fire. Worse, when some of their own shots ricocheted back, they assumed they were taking return fire and unleashed an even-larger volley, shattering windows and alarming the whole household even further.

Aside from Lassie, who likely sounded more threatening than he was, the Maleks' only security came from Mahmoud Agha, the family's long-time driver and major-domo. The slow-driving, chain-smoking Mahmoud was prized for his honesty and loyalty, and during many years of service he had become an integral part of the family. Amir was fully confident sending Mahmoud to deliver large cash payrolls to work sites around the city and, occasionally, around the country. So, no surprise, it was Mahmoud who was standing alone, shouting at the militiamen to stop firing, when they rammed the gate with their vehicles and stormed the house.

There are, in life, two predominant categories of people. There are those who pass their whole happy lives without seeing a gun or hearing one shot—except, perhaps, in the soundtrack of the latest heist movie. And there are those who live on the edge of conflict, people who see guns every day—often in the hands of careless young men. These are people who no longer flinch when a gun is fired. The boldest roll their eyes when someone sticks an AK-47 in their face at a roadside checkpoint. Peter and Shahram would find in the next hour that they were frozen out of both categories—no longer among the innocents and, just as certainly, not yet among the fearless. In a horrifying flurry, the militiamen broke through the front door, led by a shouting mullah, one of the too-numerous self-proclaimed religious leaders who had emerged as commanders in what was increasingly understood as an "Islamic" revolution. Not unusually, this particular holy man was brandishing a pistol, and he was waving what he claimed was a warrant that authorized this intrusion and the arrest of the family. With assault rifles pointing in every direction, the militiamen seized and handcuffed Peter and Shahram, and then proceeded to ransack the house, growing excited when they found a basement vault, and agitated when it turned out to be empty.

As the militia continued their search, Amir was at work in his bedroom, dialling everyone he could think of among family, friends, revolutionary government contacts—even representatives of the local revolutionary committees that had formed in response to the Revolution—trying to determine who might be assaulting his home, and why. No one knew.

Even the mullah and his makeshift militia were confused. It soon became clear that they believed the house was a love nest belonging to the Shah's twin sister, Ashraf. The gunmen were expecting spoils, not principled resistance. Yet when the militia arrived in the master bedroom, having already dragged Peter, Shahram, and Mahmoud Agha through the household search, they found Amir, sitting cross-legged on the floor, resolute. Shahram says, "Our father was extremely brave. He said calmly, 'I am not moving. If you want to kill me, you can kill me here.'"

The tension was soon relieved by another family member who, by appearances at least, was unruffled by the threat of a gun. Amir had phoned his sister-in-law, Mehri Solhizadeh, who had connections among the revolutionaries. She, in turn, had phoned everyone she knew, including Asadollah Mobasheri, Justice Minister of the Revolutionary Government, and everyone she called—including

Mobasheri—denied any knowledge of this attack. So, she drove to the house, where she arrived fearless and ferocious. She stormed through the open front door and followed the noise up the stairs, into the master bedroom and into the face of the mullah, where she demanded to know, if the minister of justice had no complaint with Amir Malek, on whose authority was this mindless assault occurring? Who authorized this purported warrant!?

Shahram says, "She was amazing. She was like a lioness!"

The night dragged on, and it became increasingly evident that the militia were not eager to admit they had come to the wrong house, at the wrong time. It turned out that the militia were from a revolutionary committee from Lavizan, a small town north of the city that is now a suburb of Tehran. That meant they were, literally, out of their jurisdiction, which, at a time when revolutionary committees were popping up everywhere, was not necessarily an enforceable issue. But the revolutionary committee from the Maleks' neighbourhood of Elahieh was, by happenstance, based in the very next house, the abandoned home of Dr. Reza Fallah, deputy chairman of the National Iranian Oil Company. Actually, the term "revolutionary committee" suggests a degree of formal organization that didn't necessarily apply. The committee was composed mostly of members of a local soccer club that seized the home at the direction of the revolutionary leadership after Dr. Fallah fled Iran as part of the Shah's entourage. They were using it as a barrack and headquarters and, awakened by the gunfire, had rushed to the scene, still rubbing their eyes from their slumber. They, too, entered through the broken gate, walking through the open front door and into the home—in force, and with the confidence that comes from being well-armed.

The group's leader, a young man named Hosseini, spoke with Amir and the boys, and then walked up to the pistol-packing mullah from

Lavizan and said, emphatically, that he and his followers had no right to be there. And finally, at nearly four in the morning, the mullah and his crew left the house, bullet-ridden and strewn with glass, and the Maleks shaken but not cowed. Before leaving however, the mullah's militia members mentioned to Shahram that they were actually former commandos who had fought—at the behest of the Shah—to put down a communist uprising in Dhofar that the Shah had feared would spread across the Gulf of Oman to his own country. While they were battle-hardened, Shahram says, "they turned out to be really nice guys," and somewhat philosophical about the uncomfortable politics of their current position. "One of them said to me, after realizing that they had been misled by the mullah: 'You know, when the country is in the hands of mullahs, this is what you have to expect.'" And though worlds apart in their background, Shahram and Hosseini, the militia head from the revolutionary committee next door, struck up a friendship that lasted through the difficult months that followed. "One look at you boys that night and I knew you were decent people," Hosseini later told him.

It was now two months since the Shah's departure—two months into a revolution that seemed to grow *less* organized and more violent by the day—and Amir began to see how tenuous life was becoming. He moved to try to protect himself and his family. It seemed fortuitous that the first prime minister under the Revolutionary Government was Mehdi Bazargan, an HVAC engineer who, before his jump into politics, had worked with the Armeh Construction Company as a subcontractor. Amir knew that Prime Minister Bazargan was due to spend the day at the Aryamehr Stadium presiding over the celebration of Nowruz, Persian New Year. Amir was already on the guest list, so he leveraged his reputation and his knowledge of the stadium to get access to his now-influential former contractor. The prime minister greeted Amir warmly and listened with concern to the details of the previous evening. Then, he invited Amir to accompany him by helicopter back to his office, where he was hosting a reception for international dignitaries. Amir continued to press his case in the helicopter and at the reception, asking for protection, consideration, and official reassurance that his family would not be attacked again. Prime Minister Bazargan seemed supportive, and sent Amir to see Amir Entezam, a senior Cabinet minister who Bazargan promised would arrange for the Malek family's safety. But Entezam left Amir sitting in an anteroom for hours. Growing impatient, Amir decided to leave. Still convinced that he had done no wrong and therefore had no reason to be fearful, he dismissed a warning from the prime minister's staff that he should wait for an escort to his car, which Hossein Bani Assadi, the company's land agent, had driven over from the stadium. Amir picks up the story in his memoir:

On Kakh Avenue, twenty meters from the Prime Minister's office, I saw an Iranian-made Peykan automobile parked, and my driver gesticulating to me from a distance to stay away. I did not, however, pay any attention to his warning, and continued on my way.

As soon as I left the building, four armed men got out of the Peykan and surrounded me, trying to push me into the car. I was confident at this point that the guards from the Prime Minister's office watching the scene would come to my rescue. Counting on their help, I put up a resistance and tried to fight off my attackers who repeatedly battered me on the head with the butt of their guns. Nevertheless, I stood my ground in such a way that the struggle lasted for quite a while. My shirt was torn, and the new suit that I had worn for Nowruz was stained with blood.

In plain view of the prime minister's guard, Amir's captors bundled him into the car and took him to yet another revolutionary committee, which convened an instant trial and posted an immediate conviction, alleging that Amir had been conspiring with the Shah's SAVAK secret police to seize the huge, twin-rotor military helicopter and kidnap the prime minister. No one cared that the charge was ridiculous. In times of political upheaval, when revolutionary players are vying for power, they don't arrest you, detain you, try you, or jail you because you have done something wrong. They do it because they can. In the case at hand, they didn't offer a credible explanation. They merely blindfolded Amir, stuffed him into another vehicle, and took him directly to the infamous Qasr Prison.

IT MAY HAVE seemed bold to sit stubbornly on the floor of his bedroom while it was being invaded, and to challenge the hapless Lavizan mullah to shoot him or leave him alone, but the logic to Amir's resistance was vindicated in the days that followed. As long as he remained within the walls of his own home, Amir had enjoyed a measure of protection. He had been surrounded by friends and family; he had options and opportunities—many reasons for hope. But from the moment that he heard the prison door slam shut behind him, he knew that his life dangled by a thread.

Qasr Prison had a ghastly history. Built as a palace in 1790 (Qasr actually translates to "palace" in Farsi), it was repurposed as a prison in 1929—heralded at the time as a modern and humane detention centre, befitting a country that still observed the legal rights of prisoners. But in the years that followed, it became known as a dungeon and interrogation chamber for enemies of the monarchy. In the early 1970s, the religious objectors to the rule of the Shah and Iran's first two "supreme leaders," the ayatollahs Ruhollah

Khomeini and Ali Hosseini Khamenei, were both imprisoned in its stark adobe-brick cells.

Amir Malek's solitary cell was damp, cold, and without a bed or chair. He took to exercising through the night to stay warm. And after another sham of a hearing on the first day, in which the revolutionaries again alleged that he was a secretly trained helicopter pilot bent on kidnapping the prime minister, Amir was left for two weeks with no visitors and no information about the likely length of his internment. He certainly had no expectation of due process. It was common knowledge that when someone's family member was dragged off to Qasr, the next phone call was likely to be an invitation to come pick up the executed prisoner's personal effects. Every evening, Amir listened as doors ground open and clanged shut, as prisoners walked by his cell and into the yard—and as "the ominous and heartbreaking sound of machinegun fire rang out." Amir later learned that the former mayor of Tehran, Gholam Reza Nikpay, who had previously been the liaison for Skidmore, Owings & Merrill on Armeh's Aryamehr Stadium project, was among those who had been shot on one of these unnerving evenings.

It was several days before the brothers were able even to confirm their father's whereabouts. "It was an absolute nightmare because we couldn't visit our dad. We didn't even know where he was. We were seeing all these executions happening, and it was very possible that he would be executed as well," Peter says. He and Shahram began contacting everyone they could think of who might be able to help, and given the failure of their father's effort to work with Prime Minister Bazargan, they turned their attention from the politically influential to religious leaders and, specifically, to the Ayatollah Mohammad Sadoughi, the imam of Friday Prayers in Amir's home city of Yazd. Ayatollah Sadoughi was credible and well-connected—he had been

appointed to the Yazd position directly by Ayatollah Khomeini—
and he was already well versed with the Maleks' record of leadership
and philanthropy in Yazd and beyond. Amir had established a huge
family charity in 1959 called the Yazd Foundation, through which he
had been building and operating hospitals, clinics, orphanages, and
schools ever since. The largest of these were in Yazd, but the foundation maintained medical facilities and free clinics in Tehran as well.

Peter, Shahram, Marjan and the boys' university friend Fred Adab
flew to Yazd and sought an audience with Ayatollah Sadoughi. Fred
remembers the scene as both stressful and comical. Sadoughi was
known as a hard-liner. While awaiting their own audience, they
learned that the last prominent businessman who had appealed to
the ayatollah's mercy had been rebuffed and executed at Qasr shortly
thereafter. So, everyone was anxious when they entered Sadoughi's
chamber and were beckoned to sit down on the floor, cross-legged in
the usual style. It was a style unfamiliar to two young men who had
grown up in England, and Shahram sat, instead, with his legs extending out in front, earning a scowl from the ayatollah and a scolding
from Fred, who kept whispering, "You can't sit like that!"

Shahram says, "It was like a scene from [the movie] *Gladiator*."
Amir's life hung in the balance: thumbs up, he would live; thumbs
down...

But Sadoughi remembered their father fondly. He knew much of
the Yazd Foundation's good works and he said that Amir had "never
turned down anyone I sent to him for help." Thumbs up! Sadoughi
went further to call Khomeini's son, Ahmad Khomeini, to vouch for
Amir. The family delegation left Yazd in great spirits, expecting that
their father would be free by the time they returned to Tehran.

It was a vain hope. Many more days passed as the politics of the
moment became both clearer and murkier. Every time they thought

they had won their father's release, some other revolutionary group would step in and block the door. Even within the walls of Qasr Prison, there were competing factions: guards of the old order; sympathizers with the Mojahedin-e-Khalq, the militant organization that had been advocating for the Shah's overthrow since 1965; as well as the inexperienced and not-always-influential officials from the new Revolutionary Government.

After Amir had been held for twenty-four days and was, by his own account, "approaching the end of what I could psychologically bear," yet another mullah came to the rescue. In the previous couple of years, Amir and Mahin had forged a quite close relationship with an enlightened young cleric named Jazaeri, who had led them on their trip to Mecca the previous year. Jazaeri, in turn, was close to the Ayatollah Anvari, a man with sufficient influence to walk into Qasr Prison without fear of anyone standing in his way. He entered the prison, commanded the jailers to open Amir's cell, and then marched him out, through every section and checkpoint, and into the hands of his waiting family.

FROM THAT DAY forward, the Maleks walked free without ever feeling free. As a condition of his release, Amir had been forced to pay a bond of one million tomans—equal then to about US$150,000—and he had to surrender his passport, but there were no other restrictions on his movements. Given the damage to their home—and the unwanted high profile of that location—the family moved into the home of some relatives, the better to stay out of view.

In the weeks that followed, Mahin and her daughters returned from Europe, where they had been during the whole of Amir's imprisonment. Peter and Shahram had not told her that Amir had been jailed, making one excuse after another as to why he wasn't in touch or available for a phone call: he was travelling for work; or perhaps he was skiing. This was typical behaviour from the family, who often tried to shield Mahin from bad news. So Mahin had learned of her husband's detention when she arrived home—from a newspaper story announcing that he had been released. Asked in an interview for this book about the impact of that discovery, she offers a small shrug and an arched eyebrow, and says she was more surprised than anything— and then relieved that it ended well.

It was a strange and uneasy time. Tehran, which had been a free-wheeling European-style city, was suddenly the capital of an Islamic republic—at times locked down, at times noisy with continuing demonstrations. But while the nightclubs were closed and the sale of liquor was banned, you could still get a bottle of Johnnie Walker Black Label delivered to your door, day or night. The wealthy and influential still partied, even if the Maleks chose not to.

It was increasingly obvious that Amir was still a target, in danger of being seized once more and accused, again and incorrectly, of having been close to the Shah. Friends kept urging him to leave the country, even if it meant forfeiting the $150,000 bond, but he was still blocked from travel. By a quirk of fortune, however, he won an audience with the new attorney general, Mehdi Hadavi. The meeting was arranged through Hadavi's son, a classmate of Amir's eldest daughter, Marjan, who was by this point enrolled in the same Harvard-based ICMS MBA program that Shahram had taken five years earlier.

Amir didn't expect much—the wheels of government were grinding slowly in this early revolutionary period—but he was grateful for any opportunity that might arise from the meeting. He was surprised that Hadavi's main concern was to support Armeh's continued operation. The Revolution had stalled the Iranian economy, and the government was concerned that work might grind to a halt at the Parc des Princes and Vanak Park projects. Amir told the attorney general that the biggest problem was finding expert help. Many of the engineers, architects, and specialists needed for such a project were ex-pats who had returned to their home countries at the outbreak of the Revolution. The only way to get them to return, Amir said, would be to go meet them in Europe and start the recruiting process afresh. Without hesitation, Hadavi said: "Fine. Go to Europe. Bring them back." And with that permission, and passport in hand, Amir boarded a plane to Paris the next day, with no intention of returning right away but no concept that he would never again set foot in the beloved land of his birth.

Peter went next. Amir had hoped that his own departure would take the focus off the family, but the spotlight soon shifted onto his eldest son, now the senior official in a family business that was sufficiently large and influential that the Revolutionary Government was monitoring its every move. In July 1979, with work at Vanak Park now at a standstill and unlikely to begin again anytime soon, Peter appealed to the revolutionary authorities for permission to go to France for a follow-up operation on the retina that had been detached years earlier in the King's College rugby game. The authorities accepted the explanation and allowed him to leave.

That left Shahram, still years from his thirtieth birthday, in direct control of the family business and in immediate and daily command at their largest still-active development project, Parc des Princes. Mahin stayed for several more months, but she and Shahram's three sisters ultimately left for Paris as well, at which point, a lonely Shahram moved into the Hyatt Regency Hotel—the safest convenient spot near the Parc des Princes job site.

Armeh had sold many of the Parc des Princes units in a pre-sale, beginning as early as 1975–76. Even from his distant vantage in Paris, Amir was determined to keep his commitment to the buyers—who, by

Iranian law (which is based on French condominium law), had been required to put down regular deposits and continue with a series of payments as construction proceeded, with the final payment being made upon delivery of the unit. The slow progress further cemented the family's good reputation, even if it also put them at continuing risk. "People would try occasionally to take us hostage," Shahram says, in a tone that, even decades later, sounds surprisingly matter of fact. It's as if he finally got bored with staring into the barrel of a gun.

On one occasion, a group of armed Air Force militiamen rolled up in American military vehicles that they had clearly confiscated when US military advisors had fled the country after the Shah's overthrow. The militiamen demanded the keys to all the apartments of the Parc des Princes project. This wasn't the first time they'd made the request, and they were becoming increasingly frustrated by Shahram's refusal. This time, they shouted at Shahram, demanding to know why he should have ownership of hundreds of apartments when there were people like them who had none. And when Shahram tried to explain again that the units were, in fact, already sold, the militiamen said they were taking him away.

By this time a large crowd of Parc des Princes workers and contractors had gathered around to hear this exchange, which was happening on one of the main streets fronting the project, and they would have none of it. At a time when most other construction projects had been closed down for lack of financing, or because the principals had fled the country, the construction workers were grateful to the Maleks for keeping the project alive. To both Shahram and the militia's surprise, the workers rushed to Shahram's defence, and they found a surprising argument to throw at the would-be kidnappers. "They surrounded the militia on the street and started shouting that I couldn't leave before paying everyone for their work," says Shahram. In point of fact, Armeh was completely up to date with its payments, at Parc des Princes and elsewhere. But it was a surprisingly effective gambit—and from a surprising source. The two men leading this group were a cement and stucco contractor named Ojaghzadeh and a painting contractor named Esmail Sabraz, both from the Azerbaijan province of Iran and reportedly communist sympathizers in their younger days. Yet, these two men first led the defence and then came to Shahram afterward and apologized for any perceived slight for shouting at him in that way and implying that he was behind on their pay. It was, they said, just the first thing they could think of to save Shahram from being taken away. The militia backed down, nervous about being surrounded by over a hundred workers, and from then on, the contractors and workers organized a daily escort to see Shahram home safely.

One of Shahram's tasks in the following months was to recover Amir's $150,000 bond, which the government said it had "released," but which it never actually handed over. Shahram bounced from one unhelpful authority figure to the next, all of whom assured him that he was free to collect the money—just not here, just not now. Finally, Shahram was given a time and place: Evin Prison, a jail that was even more ghastly than Qasr. Evin had been built in 1972 as a detention centre designed to house 320 people, mostly prisoners awaiting trial. By 1979, the prison's population had ballooned to more than 1,500, and it had become a revolutionary administrative centre as well as a dreaded house of detention.

Evin is only ten minutes north of the Parc des Princes. "It's a really pleasant neighbourhood," Shahram says—so the trip was quick to start. But once there, he found himself being directed deeper and deeper into the bowels of the jail. At some point, as he was waiting outside the accounting office, he was approached, roughly, by a stern young man, who said, "Are you Shahram Malek?" When Shahram said yes, the fellow said, "Don't move!" and went off, deeper into the jail. Looking around his unforgiving surroundings and contemplating the time his father had so recently spent in Qasr, for no reason other than being a Malek, Shahram thought better of the circumstances and eased back out the way he had come. He didn't know then that the $150,000 was a very small part of the family fortune that would ultimately fall forfeit.

Another crisis erupted some months later when a small group of condominium owners banded together and started demanding their money back. The would-be owners were already unhappy because of the earlier delay for seismic upgrading, and with a post-revolutionary drop in the real estate market, they wanted to break their contracts, take the money, and run. Beginning with the departure of the Shah himself, and accelerating through this first revolutionary year, a great many wealthy Iranians were leaving the country or, at the very least, trying to get money out of the country in case they had to flee. The buyers began by harassing Shahram, in spite of the company's assurances that it was doing everything possible to complete the project quickly and in accordance with their contracts. The buyers next went to the local revolutionary committee, demanding Shahram's arrest. The scene devolved into such disorder that someone on the committee fired a gun into the air to disperse the seemingly well-to-do and unrevolutionary-looking buyers. But then the revolutionary committee went to Shahram, who again explained the situation. Armeh had been using the funds, together with construction financing, appropriately and according to the conditions of payment, to build the project, in the process employing hundreds of workers and contractors. The best result for everyone would be to keep the project moving, even if machine operators could sometimes hear gunfire over the noise of construction. The revolutionary committee seemed to accept this logic.

The begrudging buyers and Parc des Princes ultimately agreed to mediation. They chose a consulting engineer named Hossein Daftarian, who was influential and admired by all parties, as their mediator. The meeting began as Shahram feared it would, with the buyers complaining bitterly about the delays and the apparent decline in value that had been caused by the Revolution. Daftarian, small in stature but large in reputation, listened intently and then surprised everyone by responding in a barely contained fury. Turning on the buyers, he stormed, "You should be ashamed!" At a time when every developer in the city had shut down and/or left the country, Daftarian pointed out this young man had worked without interruption and was on the eve of delivering some of the best new product in the city.

Armeh persevered to complete one last exemplary project and hand over all the units to the purchasers, even if the final cash flow and return of equity to the family never occurred. In addition, the Maleks had to abandon the apartments at Parc des Princes that Amir had set aside for his children, including five penthouses and several other luxury residences, plus the completed retail centre. But they were proud that despite seemingly unsurmountable obstacles, Parc des Princes was the only major project to be completed in Tehran during the revolutionary period.

While all this was going on, Amir was growing ever more anxious for the safety of his youngest son. As soon as Shahram had seen the project to completion and handed units over to the buyers, Amir phoned and said, simply, "I want you to leave." Shahram booked a ticket and—according to the custom of the day—sent his passport, through the airline, to the airport for processing. But before he could make the flight, he got the call: his passport was being held. He went to the airport, regardless, only to be directed to the prime minister's office, where he was greeted by an unshaven, flip-flop-wearing university student. This twenty-something gatekeeper named Tavakoli told Shahram that his travel document had been confiscated and that he couldn't leave the country, saying only that, as the last member of the Malek family remaining in Iran, "We need you to stay while we do more research."

Peter, who was in Paris with his parents, says, "Our father was the kind of person for whom nothing is impossible." Amir tried everything to find a way for Shahram to leave Iran, including investigating the options for an overland trip through the wilderness and mountains north of Tehran, across the border, and into Turkey. Ultimately, however, no one thought that was a good idea. Given the influence of Islamic clergymen, the family members got their hopes up when a senior ayatollah offered a consultation, but his recommendation fell short of their expectations. He told Shahram to pray five times a day and "the way will open."

Surprisingly, though, a way *did* open. A friend of longstanding called Shahram with a risky but interesting proposal. The friend, an Iranian who had grown up in the UK, had come to Iran after university and had thrived. He had a brother the same age as Shahram who had never set foot in the country. The friend offered to take Shahram to a notary in his ancestral home, the southern Iranian oil capital of Masjed Soleyman, where they would present Shahram as the brother who, having returned from the UK, now wanted to claim his Iranian birth certificate. The plan worked.

Even armed with a new identity, Shahram could not travel, because the brother had never completed his mandatory military service or received an exemption. Shahram's friend had both anticipated and planned for this next challenge. He took Shahram next to the nearest army barracks, where they presented Shahram as too incompetent to serve. The friend had said to Shahram, "Just act dumb." Shahram merely sat silent through the ensuing interview, ignoring questions, and staring into the middle distance. Remarkably, it worked again. Shahram says, "It was a scary experience, and my friend was the real hero."

There remained a couple of other difficult steps. First, Shahram needed to apply for a passport in this new identity, which meant dropping off an application, complete with his new birth certificate—and Shahram's own photo!—at the government office where his original confiscated passport remained somewhere on file. In an age before facial recognition software, it seemed a reasonable hope that no one would be conducting extensive photo comparisons before approving new passports, but this step added to a growing sense of risk.

Even after clearing that hurdle, however, Shahram still had to run the gauntlet of police and security officers at the airport. As everywhere in Tehran by this time, there were factions. The police once loyal to the Shah were still in place, and they were duplicated by a new contingent of revolutionary committees. The two groups hated one another. This worked to Shahram's advantage: his school friend had a connection among the Shah's former police, a handsome young officer who was willing to give Shahram a pass and who promised to let him know if he had been recognized by anyone in the revolutionary force. Still, Shahram's heart was pounding as he prepared for the day. Even with a rough new beard that he had grown for the occasion, he still had a recognizable face. He had spent the previous weeks signing over the recently completed units at the Parc des Princes to a host of new owners, many of whom were regular travellers; these were exactly the kinds of people who might call out his real name as they passed him in the airport.

Shahram's last layer of protection was an Italian visa under his new identity, which he had secured through the good graces of the Italian consul general, who was renting the Maleks' now-repaired hilltop villa. Shahram hoped that the visa, as much as the careful preparations and the new passport, would secure his passage through the gate and onto the plane for Rome, after which he could journey on to Paris. At 5:30 a.m. on a sunny August morning in 1980, a full year after his father had left the country, Shahram, too, climbed for one last time into a car driven by the loyal Mahmoud Agha and decamped for the Mehrabad Airport. He had slicked back his hair, grown a light, revolutionary beard, and donned a pair of glasses, hoping he still looked like his passport photo while not sufficiently like himself that he would be recognized by friend or foe. He passed through the airport's marble entranceway and retrieved his passport at the Alitalia desk, and then headed to passport control. Then it was past the Revolutionary Guards, whose only interest seemed to be whether he had contraband in his luggage.

The journey passed in a blur. Shahram was too tense even to feel relief once the plane cleared the tarmac. The full realization came when he landed in Rome. His father was waiting and, Shahram says, "so relieved!" They went directly to the luxurious rooms of the Excelsior Hotel on Via Veneto and stayed there for what Shahram still describes as "the best three days ever! Dad was happy and relaxed, and we met many of his Italian and Iranian friends in Rome. We went to nice restaurants and spent the evenings together in Via Veneto cafes near the hotel. Despite having left all his money, assets, buildings, and life behind in Iran, he had a positive energy now that his last family member was safe. He was ready for the next chapter of our family life and seemed excited about it, even relishing the unknown challenges ahead."

IT'S A CURIOUS coincidence that Shahram slipped out of Tehran by a tactic similar to one used to liberate six American diplomats who had avoided capture in the November 1979 Tehran hostage taking at the US Embassy. The Americans had taken refuge in the homes of then–Canadian Ambassador to Iran Ken Taylor and John Sheardown, another Canadian Embassy official. After hiding out—at great risk to themselves and to the Canadians who harboured them—the six diplomats left Iran on January 27, 1980, as part of a fake American film crew, using counterfeit passports provided by the Canadian Embassy. The fifty-two American hostages would remain in custody for another year, winning a negotiated release only on January 20, 1981.

The whole period was both frightening and heartbreaking for the Maleks. While they had always been scrupulously apolitical—and while they originally assumed that the religious leaders of the Revolutionary Government would act modestly and responsibly, Shahram says now, "What happened to our country was very sad." Peter agrees, saying, "Iran was one of the most progressive countries in the Middle East, maybe the most progressive country." It was prosperous and peaceful, and unusual among Middle Eastern countries, it had good relations with Israel as well as Arab countries. As long as you stayed out of politics, Peter says, "you could do what you want." Shahram adds, "A woman could walk down the streets of Tehran at three o'clock in the morning and feel totally safe."

The Malek family left more than a beloved homeland. In the Parc des Princes development alone, they left thirty apartments, which they had kept for members of the extended family; five penthouses for Amir's children; and two 5,000-square-foot homes that had been designed for Peter and Shahram. The family also owned three office towers downtown, one fully rented to Pan American Oil, one to the Iran state railway, and a third, the 14-storey Paziran Building, that had served as their corporate headquarters, which they also left behind. There were large landholdings, including prime parcels in excess of 100 acres in Farahzad in north Tehran; about 500 acres in Ahwaz in southern Iran, and in Bandar Abbas on the Strait of Hormuz; and the

8-acre Vanak Park site under construction in Tehran, to name a few. Armeh was the largest road paving and construction company in Iran, and Amir had a habit of buying up still-affordable parcels when the company got a contract to build a new road. There was also construction equipment that, even in the pre-inflationary dollars of the day, was worth many millions. Unlike in Canada, where large contractors and developers often subcontract much of their work, a big player in Iran had to be able to provide all the necessary gear, which meant owning trucks, bulldozers, tower cranes, concrete batching plants— everything you'd need to finish a big job.

Among the family's personal possessions, they also left behind their big house in Tehran, which still sits proudly on a 1-acre hilltop promontory in the city's best neighbourhood, and which last changed hands at a price that translates to something in excess of CA$50 million. And there was their summer home on 25 waterfront acres on the Caspian Sea. Emotionally, at least, none of it was ever "abandoned." Peter and Shahram say that their father always planned to return, to claim what was his—which, of course, was not to be. But in 1980, they were safe in their apartment in Paris, and with enough money in European banks to live comfortably for a couple of years without having to immediately find work. And against all that loss, Shahram says, "our father seemed almost excited. He really looked forward to the challenge of starting again from scratch."

THE NEW WORLD

In 1979, as the stern, hostile face of Ayatollah Ruhollah Khomeini began to represent Iran in the Western world, Amir Malek found that the warm welcome he had always enjoyed abroad was transforming into "antipathy and disdain." Effectively banished from his own country, he nevertheless carried the stain of the very revolutionaries who had shot up his home, devastated his businesses, and, ultimately, seized even the buildings that he had committed to charity. He had no choice but to begin again. But where? And how?

Freshly settled in Paris, Amir put those questions to Jean Lefebvre, the principal of L'Entreprise Jean Lefebvre, the construction and engineering firm with which Armeh had done so much work in Iran, and where Peter had interned only a few years earlier. Lefebvre's advice: go west! He said Europe was too crowded, too bound by its own histories and relationships. As Peter recalls, Lefebvre recommended that they go to America, where an outsider had a better chance starting from scratch. Peter remembers Lefebvre's exact words: "In America, anybody can be successful."

If you were thinking about North America, "the natural thing" was to think about the United States of America, Peter says, adding, "Who was thinking about Canada at that time?" For the Maleks, every image of Canada came from history books and travel brochures, all of which concentrated on Mounties in red serge jackets or sweeping mountain vistas, shot from the dome car of a passenger train.

Amir dispatched his eldest son to the US for a fact-finding tour that began in New York City. There, Peter was surprised to find "ultimate decadence." With friends who were already living in the city, he went dancing at Studio 54 and spent an evening as a bemused witness in Plato's Retreat, the famous swingers' club in the Ansonia Hotel, upstairs from the gay bathhouse where Bette Midler rose to fame singing raunchy show tunes with Barry Manilow accompanying on a grand piano.

After four or five days of New York–level partying, Peter set off across the country, intent on working through a list of locations and business opportunities that his father had been researching in advance. He got a warm welcome in Nashville, Tennessee—as a potential investor of substance, "They gave me the keys to the city!"—and then he moved on to look at properties in Sarasota, Florida. Amir then joined him for visits to Houston, Texas; Tucson, Arizona; and then San Francisco, Los Angeles, and San Diego, in California. Nothing caught their fancy. So, when Amir returned to Paris toward the end of the year, he suggested that Peter go to Seattle, where he knew a couple of well-established architects who might be able to help the family get a foothold.

The opportunities looked promising, even if the timing was anything but right. Interest rates were rising toward 20 percent and everything in the real estate world was more difficult than it had ever been. Peter bought a condo on the twenty-fifth floor of one of only two prominent residential buildings in Seattle at the time. It was beautiful, with an endless view over Puget Sound, but condos were new, and Seattleites were uneasy with this unfamiliar ownership model. "People thought it was a crazy thing to do." Peter registered a new construction company, had a couple of false starts, and didn't wind up building anything. Instead, in less than a year, he says, "I decided to just get a job." He looked up and down the coast for opportunities and wound up applying to Cahill Construction in San Francisco, a large firm with a particular expertise in building high-rises. Peter hoped to learn more about how the construction and development industry functioned in North America, saying, with a smile, "It was a little bit like industrial espionage." He rented an apartment on San Francisco's renowned Russian Hill and settled into a happy life.

In Paris, meanwhile, Amir was enjoying an afternoon stroll one day when he happened upon a lineup of people on the sidewalk along Avenue Montaigne in the 8th arrondissement. He stopped to ask someone what the attraction was, and they said that this was the location of the Canadian Embassy; they were waiting to apply for visas. This, Amir thought, could be the answer to the riddle of his family's future: not America, which was promising but had not caught his fancy; not France, which was beloved in the family, but, according to his advisor, not promising; but Canada, a place with North American opportunity and stability and a potential home for all. Never one to hesitate, Amir joined the line and by the time he returned to his apartment, he had applications for the whole family.

The Government of Canada accepted Amir, Mahin, and four of their adult children—even Shahram, who, having left Iran with a counterfeit passport, was technically approved as a refugee. Following the advice of friends and counsellors who said Vancouver was the very best choice of Canadian cities, Amir and Mahin landed there in February 1981, and bought a house on Palmerston Avenue in West Vancouver and an apartment for Shahram on Folkestone Way, a stunning location overlooking the whole city and a two-minute walk from one of the region's most famous restaurants, Salmon House on the Hill.

Shahram travelled from Paris to Vancouver in May, stopping to visit school friends living in Montreal and Toronto. "I loved both cities," he says. They were cosmopolitan and bustling, with evening concerts and lunches at sidewalk cafés in the warm late-spring sun. He was still excited about coming west. His friends preached the glory of Vancouver and promised he would be startled by the beauty of the mountains and the water. And when he arrived, he might have been startled—if he could have seen either. Driving over the Lions Gate Bridge to the home his parents had bought for him in West Vancouver, all he saw was rain and fog. He says, "I've never seen anything like it since. I thought: 'This is a horrible mistake.'" He arrived on Folkestone Way to a beautiful apartment without a stick of furniture—mired in a shroud of cloud that obscured the whole view.

The sun broke through eventually and with it came Shahram's first brush with an outrageously welcoming Canadian. Laffin Tompkins, a six-foot-five insurance executive originally from the Maritimes, appeared at Shahram's door, begging forgiveness in advance for the disruption that might follow as the Tompkins had the floors redone in the condo upstairs. The two fell into conversation and Laffin invited Shahram to meet his wife, Patricia, and their four children. In the coming days, Laffin introduced Shahram to anyone else in the complex he might find interesting—a list that included a subsequent development-industry star named Michael Audain. Life got even better for Shahram with the arrival of his sister and new roommate, Marjan, and a gorgeous selection of Italian Cassina furniture that Mahin had picked out for the apartment on the Boulevard Saint-Germain in Paris.

To Shahram, Laffin encompassed everything good about Canada. He was friendly, kind, and loved British Columbia. He told Shahram that he'd come to the best place in the world, and he always wanted to help. "There was a genuineness to Laffin that made him and his family very special to us."

Amir rented space in a shared office downtown in the Rogers Building at Granville and Pender, and he incorporated a new company, Armeco. Then he gave Shahram his marching orders for the weeks and months to come. They would begin as he had in Iran, seeking out construction projects on contract and building a new business from there.

Amir had already given his sons and daughters some general guidance on adapting to their new environment. He told them that in Europe and the Middle East, people would judge you by your family—by who you were. In North America, he said, they would judge by your actions, not your status. So, he told them, "Never talk about what you had or what you *did*. Talk about what you *do*."

While setting up in Vancouver, he gave more specific instructions to Shahram. He said: get in the car and drive to every municipality in the region; go to every municipal hall and talk to the planners. Find out what they want and what they need. Ask for their official community plans. If the Maleks were to begin again, they would have to take whatever construction projects were available until they built the local knowledge—and the equity—that would be necessary to break into development. Setting out on his first foray, Shahram was thinking that this was an effective make-work project—that it was a good way of keeping someone busy. But he found there was much to learn—and that, "people were so nice and so helpful."

Amir found an advisor in the influential tax lawyer, art collector, and philanthropist Jacques Barbeau. Shahram says that Barbeau "looked a bit like William Holden, the movie star. My dad wanted to find out what we needed to do in Vancouver, how we should act, what we should expect." One of the first questions Amir asked Barbeau was whether the family should abbreviate or anglicize their name. They had been admitted to Canada under Malekyazdi, the formality of which was understood in Iran but seemed awkward in Canada. "What about just using Malek?" they asked. Barbeau said no. He said that Canada is different from the United States, more enthusiastically multicultural. As evidence, he pointed out that the federal finance minister of the day was named Don Mazankowski; surely, then, Canadians would have no difficulty with Malekyazdi!

These stories reveal two consistencies, two things that might also seem familiar in the histories of other immigrant families who found prosperity in this new land. The first is that Amir never tired of seeking advice. He told Shahram to call local contractors and developers of all types and sizes and ask for a meeting—to ask them how they do business. And make notes! Shahram always wondered, "Why would they tell us?" But he called one company after another and learned the second consistent trend: most were willing to share a coffee, and to share their intelligence. The owner of a small but long-standing local construction firm turned the tables—and began quizzing Amir and Shahram about their own experience. On hearing that Amir had only recently lost a company that, at its height, had employed thousands of people—and hearing the extent of the work that Armeh had done in Iran—their new Canadian advisor looked across the desk and said, "What are you doing here? I should be asking *you* for advice."

Among the kindest of strangers in those early days was Amalio DeCotiis, the eldest brother in another multi-generational immigrant family that became successful in real estate development. In the early 1980s, Amalio's company, VIAM, specialized in wood-frame apartment buildings. At Jacques Barbeau's request, he agreed to teach Shahram the specifics and peculiarities of the Vancouver construction and real estate market. Amalio would drive with Shahram to one project after another and walk through, taking note of the progress and the problems. "I learned so much from him," Shahram says. A big man with a big heart who drove "a big American car," Amalio's Italian accent was so thick that it took Shahram many days to grow confident that he fully understood the master's lessons. The effort paid off handsomely. "He [Amalio] made everything simple. He took away the mystery of construction in Vancouver." Sometimes, in the middle of these teaching days, Amalio would drive Shahram to his favourite Italian restaurant on Commercial Drive, where Amalio was greeted like royalty and feted with what seemed like an endless selection of specialties. When Shahram said, "Wow, these guys really like you," Amalio smiled, shrugged, and said, "No, no. They're going to overcharge me for all this later."

Even later, when others were edging into the lucrative condo market, Shahram asked Amalio why he continued to build only rentals. Amalio said, "I want to keep what I build." And when Shahram suggested there could be more money to be made in the condo and high-rise markets, the master offered a response that Shahram still remembers precisely: "What can I do with more money? Can I eat more food? Can I drink more wine?" It's an old-fashioned notion.

While Shahram and Peter were serving out their separate apprenticeships, Amir was leading the campaign to secure a new construction contract. On the surface, this seemed to be a straightforward prospect. As Jean Lefebvre had promised, there were few apparent barriers to entry in the Vancouver market. In Iran, Shahram says, you needed to own all the elements of production if you hoped to bid on a project of any significance—"you needed to own your own construction equipment, your concrete plant and your asphalt plant. You had to have your own tower cranes." In Canada, you just needed to post a performance bond (a form of security that a contractor would forfeit if they failed to complete), buy the insurance, and engage subtrades that could do the work. Given the Maleks' experience and background, those were surmountable obstacles. So, Armeco bid on a whole series of small-to-medium-size construction contracts—all with no success. Their bids were consistently too high.

Amir directed that they should prepare a bid for the next project without including any margin for profit. They needed to break into the market, and as an engineer with long experience and a well-honed creative streak, he was confident that, once they won a job, he would use innovative construction methods to save money and time. So confident, in fact, that they prepared a bid at what they calculated to be a $50,000 loss.

The BC Place parkade was a $1-million contract on a tight schedule. A 5-storey parking garage topped by a plaza connecting BC Place Stadium to the Yaletown neighbourhood to the west, it had to be completed in less than a year, in time for Queen Elizabeth II's March 1982 visit to the city for the inauguration of the 65,000-seat BC Place sports and entertainment venue. Given the lowball offer, they won the bid, somewhat to the puzzlement of Phillips Barratt, the consulting engineers who represented the owner, Crown corporation BC Place, and who had expected to be dealing with a proven local contractor.

Amir directed all hands to the task. Shahram was already in place and Marjan was busy crunching the numbers, but as soon as construction started Amir also summoned Peter, saying he was needed, immediately, in Vancouver.

Peter says now that he was not pleased. "I loved San Francisco."

"Yes," Shahram says, "and you hated Vancouver."

But he came, eventually, to love Vancouver too, and together the family proved to be unstoppable. Phillips Barratt resolutely refused to accept any of Amir's innovations. There would be no prefabricated technology from Dywidag, the well-known German company, which could have improved the budget by cutting construction time. And when the Maleks pointed out that there were extra features that were driving up the costs, their lead engineer, Clark Cunningham, invited the Malek team to take it up with the principals representing BC Place, Louis van Blankenstein and Paul Brinton. But Cunningham also offered a caution: he said that van Blankenstein was "a table thumper," who could make such negotiations uncomfortable. On the bright side, Brinton was also a big fan of Japanese food. So, Shahram says, "We had a nice lunch with Paul and Clark—it was a good introduction to Japanese cuisine and to ways of doing business in our new country. But we didn't get very far on the extras."

So, the parkade, already underbid, was an expensive adventure. But it immediately turned the previously unknown Armeco into a proven local provider. Come the third week in March 1982, when Her Majesty Queen Elizabeth II stood before clearing skies, celebrating the first domed stadium in Canada and offering the world an early invitation to what would become Vancouver's global coming-out party—Expo 86—she likely had no idea that she was standing over 5 storeys of parking only recently and expertly completed. But others knew, and Armeco—and the whole Malek family—had a toehold in the new world.

A toehold, however, is not a home. And Peter, especially, was feeling the pressure of being a nomad, but was still uncertain about this move to Vancouver. Even while doing most of their growing up in

England, he and Shahram had always felt secure in their identity. They were rooted in Iran, conscious always of having a home and a loving family. Whether travelling back and forth or enjoying one of their frequent family vacations in Europe, they had moved through the world with pride and self-assurance. "The Iranian passport was a good one to have," Peter says. It was welcomed everywhere, usually without question and almost always without a visa.

"But," Peter says, "after the Revolution, you couldn't go any-where." So, the idea of a passport became something of an obsession. Having faced down gunmen in his own home, having departed his own country, at risk and great sacrifice, he longed for some symbol of security—of status. Early in what still felt like a period of exile, while living in San Francisco, he had hired a lawyer to investigate the options for gaining citizenship in another country. The lawyer advised that the easiest and least-expensive option could be found on the Caribbean island nation of Dominica, where citizenship was, in effect, available for a fee. So, Peter applied. Then, while working at Cahill Construction in San Francisco, on the large mixed-use Opera Plaza project on Van Ness Avenue, he got a Green Card, securing his right to work in the United States. Actual citizenship followed in January 1983, and with this promising new status, he felt he was fitting in nicely. It all made the move to Vancouver even more disruptive and unsettling.

IT'S HARD TO imagine that an act of kindness—of professionalism and goodwill—could sow the seeds of future devastation, but it's clear from the way they tell the story today that the Maleks are rue-ful about the effects of the excellent treatment they received from the City of Vancouver on their next major piece of work. The call was for a complicated extension of Cordova Street west of Granville Street. It required the construction of a functional bridge at street level, with ramps woven into the middle lanes to provide access and egress to a subterranean street network connecting to the waterfront. It's the kind of work that would have been challenging at the edge of town, in a greenfield development, and even more challenging on this site, which was adjacent to one of the densest parts of the city and would involve a huge excavation beside the Sinclair Centre at Cordova and Howe streets. Even after the successful completion of the BC Place parkade, it was probably nervy for Armeco even to bid on such a project; it was three times larger and so much more prominent in the public eye. No matter, says Shahram. "Our father was not afraid."

Armeco's bid was the lowest. But Eric West, the City of Vancouver engineer in charge of vetting proponents, was moving cautiously. Armeco had done a creditable job on the stadium parkade, but this was no place for a high-profile disaster. So, he invited the principals to come in for a meeting to give him a better sense of whether they had the right stuff. Amir was in Paris, so Peter and Shahram took the meeting, setting up a moment of awkwardness for everyone. By the brothers' description, West was "old school and correct." In the months that followed, Shahram says they would find him "meticulous and fair, really delightful." But at the moment of their introduction, he was all skepticism and challenge. After all, it said in their bidding materials that Armeco had thirty-five years of experience with major public works, and here he was, sitting across from two young men hardly out of their twenties. Looking askance, he said, "Which one of you has thirty-five years' experience?" Peter and Shahram, proceeded to make their case for corporate competence. They described Armeh's long history in Iran and they did so with sufficient fluency that West put aside his concern and set about doing everything in his power to help these upstarts succeed in a difficult, prominent, and extremely important public work.

On time, on budget, constructionally elegant, and completed with the minimum of disruption, the Cordova Street project, site-managed by the capable Hamid Rousta who became a lifelong friend, cemented Armeco's reputation as a reliable contractor. It also had a lasting impact on the Maleks, who were left with the impression that the City of Vancouver was an excellent partner—fair, reliable, and committed to the success of its associates. Notwithstanding the difficulties that would follow, they still cherish a copy of the letter that West sent on behalf of the City, on May 29, 1984, "to advise you that we are extremely satisfied with the conduct of this contract. The work has been done well and has met our schedule and has been performed within the budget."

Of course, it's always risky to use the past as a predictor of the future.

In the bids and projects to follow, the Maleks were reminded, again and again, that just because there were no insurmountable barriers to entry in the North American construction market, that didn't mean the process was easy. Sure, you didn't have to own your own concrete batching plant or tower cranes. But before you submitted your bid, which had to be complete, on time, and lower than everyone else's, you still needed to have all the pieces in place. You had to be ready with candidates for construction superintendent and foremen. You needed a reliable supply of labourers and you had to assure the availability and cost of subtrades, which meant calling for bids from them as you were preparing your bid. You also had to assemble all this information in a highly competitive environment at a time when your best and most-experienced rivals were preparing bids for the same work. And—harkening back to the now unimaginable time before computers—you had to do all this with telephones and pieces of paper. With Peter, Shahram, and Marjan all working the phones and crunching numbers, Peter says, "it was so stressful. I never really smoked, but I was always chain-smoking during this process."

Once a bid was done, they would deliver it in person, sitting-in while the bidding authority opened the tenders. This was more stressful still. There were bids they won by too wide a margin, having obviously left money on the table, and there were bids that they lost by a whisker. And, once in a while, there were projects they walked away from with some sense of relief. For example, they bid on the replacement of the Cambie Street Bridge, a huge contract that was widely regarded as a transportation linchpin in preparation for Expo 86—itself, an international transportation exhibition. The Cambie Bridge, like the Cordova extension, would have been an opportunity to demonstrate Armeco's competence in a high-profile and crucial public work. But, Peter says, "our price was really low. We were almost happy when someone else underbid us."

Still, Amir remained fearless—confident in his increasingly capable offspring and innovative in both engineering and finance. At one point, for example, he tried to convince the City of Vancouver to let Armeco build parking facilities for free directly beneath downtown streets, especially along wide swaths of Georgia and Burrard, with the money flowing back to Armeco through regular parking fees. This was years before the term "public-private partnership" had become popular. The City dismissed this innovative notion out of hand, saying those rights-of-way were reserved for too many pipes and services. The Maleks just shrugged, still confident that if such a thing can be done in Paris, where the below-ground infrastructure is even denser and older, it certainly could be done in Vancouver.

Aware of bottlenecks on the Lions Gate Bridge connecting Vancouver to the North Shore, Amir asked Shahram to propose to the government to allow Armeco to build a tunnel under the Burrard Inlet, again at its cost, to be paid for by tolls. (One of the engineers who had helped design the George Massey Tunnel under the Fraser River in 1959 made an almost identical proposal in the early 1990s—and it received an identically dismissive response.) And when the well-situated but rail-covered industrial lands on Coal Harbour in downtown Vancouver came up for sale, Amir asked Shahram to propose to Graham Stamp, then principal of CP Rail's real estate arm, Marathon, that they would buy all the lands if a fair deal could be struck. If any other Vancouver newcomer had come up with these ideas, they might have seemed like pie in the sky. But Amir had the confidence of his years of experience in doing challenging but well-researched projects, even after others had balked, or failed.

Armeh's European connections gave Armeco another edge, enabling the new Canadian company to bid credibly on jobs that a small upstart could never have considered. For example, they bid on what was then called the Annacis Island bridge—now the Alex Fraser—in concert with one of Europe's premiere engineering firms, WTB of Augsburg, Germany. They missed on the price, but by that point, no one could have doubted Armeco's seriousness as a new player. Shahram says, "Our father always said, 'If you find the right project, the money will come.'"

In the years that followed, that proved to be true. Small or large, anonymous or high profile, Armeco continued to tackle whatever was available, taking particular pleasure in projects that called for a degree of innovation and imagination. Two quirky-but-complicated Armeco challenges arose amid the preparations for Expo 86, the international exposition that would be so influential in rehabilitating the north side of Vancouver's False Creek and in bringing one of the world's most beautiful cities to international attention. Both projects read (accurately) like fodder for the pages of *The Guinness Book of World Records*. The first was to be the world's largest hockey stick; and the second, the world's tallest free-standing flagpole. Both would act as giant markers at the exposition's main entrance. The hockey stick, commissioned by the federal government, is forty times life size. The shaft and blade of the stick were fabricated in Penticton from steel-reinforced, glulam Douglas fir beams that were 3 feet by 4 feet by 205 feet long. Trucked to Vancouver in two pieces and spliced together on the grounds, the finished product weighed 62,000 pounds. It rests now outside a community centre in Duncan, on Vancouver Island, where it was barged two years after the fair.

Even thirty-five years later, the Expo hockey stick still holds the international record. Canadians have always put up a tough challenge in the hockey arena. Flagpoles, however, are a more competitive category. The 282-foot Expo 86 flagpole was overtaken as the world's tallest decades ago. The current record holder, at 560 feet, towers over King Abdullah Square in Jeddah, Saudi Arabia, and every pole in the top 10 is over 300 feet. But that hardly diminishes the achievement at the time. The Maleks' Expo pole weighs 600 tons, which makes it roughly equivalent to a long, lean railway locomotive. The concrete-and-steel base alone weighs another 300 tons. The pole also migrated after the world fair, to Guildford in the Vancouver suburb of Surrey, where the good folks at what is now the Barnes Wheaton auto dealership have taken responsibility for tending the legacy and keeping the 30-foot by 80-foot flag flying in the West Coast's windy weather. The cost of that commitment might itself be Guinness-record worthy, as flags seldom last more than a couple of months and replacements cost upward of $3,500 each.

At a more practical level, Armeco settled into a series of increasingly ambitious public works, including a large sewage treatment facility on Iona Island just north of the Vancouver International Airport, hospital expansions in Langley and Surrey, and a significant expansion of the Victoria International Airport. Guy Nylund, a Canadian-Finnish engineer, played a key role as project manager on many of these undertakings. And each new success got the fledgling enterprise closer to the Maleks' original goal of building a sufficient stake to move, once more, from construction-on-contract into development, where Armeco would finance (or arrange financing for) its own projects, carry the risk, and, if successful, reap the reward.

"SHAHRAM, YOU HAVE to sell your apartment." With that brief dictate, Amir Malek summed up the central message of an early morning phone call. A friendly agent with Sussex Realty, Klaas Van Den Bos, had pointed out a perfect development property in the Dundarave neighbourhood in West Vancouver, and the Maleks were working to assemble enough capital to launch the family's first development project since moving to Canada. This was both a dream and, for Shahram, a nightmare. The dream was Amir's: ever since he had left the Iranian city of Yazd as a child, he had longed to recreate the family compound—not just a home for himself and Mahin, but somewhere he could gather his whole extended family. This was to be Regency Place, a twenty-four-unit condominium development with main-floor commercial space, all of it just steps away from the Dundarave high street, one of West Vancouver's most desirable retail strips.

For Shahram, however, it was a bitter pill to swallow. He loved his life in the apartment, which he regarded as one of the best in the city, and based on the view alone, it would be hard to argue. The condo is perched high on the North Shore mountainside, in the exclusive British Properties. Standing before the vast picture windows, you can look east to watch the sun rise over Mount Baker or west to see it set over the Strait of Georgia, Vancouver Island, and the snow-capped mountains of the Olympic range south of the US border. Directly below—in addition to English Bay and Burrard Inlet—are the graceful spires and cables of the Lions Gate Bridge, the sprawling green darkness of Stanley Park and the glittering lights of downtown.

Yet he also understood the need to let it go. And he regarded his acquiescence as a necessary partial payment of a lifelong debt. "Because of everything our parents did for us, when they asked for something, we felt we had to agree," says Shahram. "They made us who we are. Without our father's love and guidance, our lives could have taken a much different turn. He had confidence in us. He believed we could move mountains."

This modesty and gratitude are typical of Shahram. Also typical, though, is the pause that follows. Even as Peter is chiming in to say, "I think Shahram is exaggerating *a little bit*," Shahram is looking to his older brother and saying, "... I mean at least in *my* case." They both smile.

This, too, is typical—a disagreement that doesn't become an argument. Peter and Shahram don't necessarily look like brothers, not at a passing glance. Peter, who is bigger in stature, clearly takes after his mother, Mahin. He's famous in the business world as the rock you want to avoid during a tough negotiation, but he shows little sign of that fierceness in casual conversation. Softspoken and gracious, he has a round, unfurrowed face and an easy calm, and he lets Shahram lead the conversation in such instances. Shahram, who looks more like his father, Amir, is leaner—it's no surprise to hear that he's a runner—and his dark eyes are kind, but also focused. But for all their differences, you can't watch the two business partners for long without being reminded that they are brothers. They move seamlessly, not just finishing each other's sentences but also often telling stories in harmony, weaving the narrative together clause by clause. (To have been perfectly accurate about the quotes in this book, it would have been necessary to distribute the attribution of almost every comment between them. You can be sure, even if Shahram seems to have said more in a conversation, that Peter has added, adjusted, or, in some other way, contributed to almost every statement.) Their professional skills are overlapping, thanks to Amir's teachings in construction and real estate, and complementary: Peter, the engineer, is relentless about construction issues, design details, and the sharply drawn numbers on the bottom line; Shahram, the MBA, manages business development and project design, finance, and marketing—and, when absolutely necessary, and reluctantly, public speaking. In the tactical world of teams that break into good cops and bad cops, Shahram is ever warm and accommodating, Peter ferociously precise. But their long-time (and now-retired) assistant, Helena Maurice, says that whenever one was out of town, the other would fill in perfectly—each knowing all that was essential about the other's specialties.

The two men also exhibit the balance of tension and accommodation that successful brothers learn early and practice often. They are not obviously competitive, but they hold one another to account, firing up the iPad to consult Google anytime a difference in opinion needs to be resolved. It's a boyish reaction—challenging but charming—and you can still see, plainly, the affection that inspired eight-year-old Shahram to insist that he, too, should fly to England for a school life far from home, but near his older brother.

And if there is yet any doubt as to the admiration, adoration, and gratitude they both feel toward their parents, consider that, even today, as "boys" whose own children are mostly grown, they still get in the car every day and drive from downtown to West Vancouver to have lunch with Mahin. (And if they're running late, she calls...) So, when Amir phoned Shahram, there was never a question as to whether he would sell his beloved condo, only a matter of how he could do so in the best possible way.

This also prompts the question of why Amir and company were so eager to move from the established success of their growing construction business into the riskier world of property development. Peter is unsentimental with his first answer: "The return is much better." At least, it is in Canada. In Iran, where you had to own almost every component of a construction business to bid on contracts, the competition was less intense and the markup correspondingly higher. In Canada, with fewer barriers to entry, there were many more people bidding on jobs, often based on corresponding bids from the same subcontractors, so there was much less room for differentiation. The general contractor who won was often the one that had shaved his own profit closest to the bone.

In development, on the other hand, you create your own opportunity. Rather than scanning the pages of the *Journal of Commerce*, looking for upcoming work and competing for the right to participate, you can leverage your own creativity—and take your own risks—building projects of your own conception and design. So, Peter says, "You can make a huge amount, or lose a huge amount." (An Olympic pause follows.)

Regency Place, by the Maleks' earlier and later standards a modest building tucked discretely into its West Vancouver neighbourhood, was an economic success—and Shahram got a new apartment. If he liked it less than his perch higher up the hill, at least he was closer to his parents.

EVERYTHING IN LIFE is not necessarily a rehearsal for something else. You don't always do something because you are trying, specifically, to hone the skills you will need to accomplish some ambitious future endeavour. Sometimes you pick a project for the potential profit—sometimes purely for the pleasure. But what you do today is still practice for tomorrow. In any pursuit, you build expertise. You get in the habit. That explains why some developers find themselves in a niche. They build suburban single-family homes, or 4-storey wood-frame apartments, or mid-rise concrete condo buildings, or mixed-use towers. Such projects don't need to be unimaginative, cookie-cutter repetitions to give themselves away as the work of a particular developer. You can often recognize a certain signature.

But it would be hard to ascribe a typological consistency to the next generation of Malek developments. In the twenty-four years between 1984 and 2008, they completed more than twenty-six development projects across a startling range. There were shopping centres (Sunwood Square in Coquitlam, Windsor Square in White Rock, Sunshine Village in Delta), low-rise condos and townhomes (St. James Gate in Port Coquitlam, St. Andrews at Deer Lake in Burnaby, Brownstone in Vancouver), and high-rise residential towers, including a whole community arrayed around a grand formal garden (City-in-the-Park in Burnaby). There was a one-off heritage restoration (The Province Building in Vancouver) and, in a rare thematic period, two of West Vancouver's most luxurious residential projects (Edgewater and the Water's Edge). Add in the big, mixed-use commercial and residential building with a luxury hotel (L'Hermitage in Vancouver) and a conference centre in Nanaimo and you begin to get a sense of the range. If you were looking for consistency, you might notice it in the brothers' fondness for the names of English hotels and neighbourhoods they remembered from their days at school: Claridges, The Savoy, Mayfair, Belgravia. Carlton, which they used on two buildings, was the name of their parents' favourite hotel in Cannes, France; Lumiere, one they liked in Paris.

You also would notice the consistency in quality. Malek buildings are noticeably among the nicest in their neighbourhoods. Shahram says, "Our dad always said, 'Whatever you do, do it with passion.'" So, the brothers engaged great architects and then built the kinds of buildings they themselves would like to live in. Whether it reflects modesty or some lack of presumptuousness, they don't seem to have been driven by an egomaniacal vision to put their stamp on the city. Their ambition was more immediate—and more practical. "We try to make a difference," Shahram says, Peter adding, "Besides, if you build it right, people will come to your project rather than go to someone else's."

The Maleks proved themselves to be astute competitors and accommodating partners. Soon after finishing Regency Place, they began assembling land in Coquitlam on which they would ultimately build the Sunwood Square shopping centre, and they discovered that another developer, Rod Schroeder, was also assembling land in the same neighbourhood—and for a similar purpose. Schroeder was a cousin and mentor to Ian Gillespie, who went on to form Westbank Corp, now one of the largest development practices in Vancouver and an increasingly influential player in the Toronto and Seattle markets as well. Gillespie remembers the Maleks as "a class act" from the very outset. Rather than squabble over the property, the Maleks teamed up with Schroeder's group to form a joint venture—a convenience because Schroeder himself had a long-standing relationship with Safeway, which would be a highly valuable main tenant in the new centre. As a condition of their partnership, the Maleks insisted that their construction firm, Armeco, would get the actual construction contract. Schroeder resisted at first but ultimately conceded. When the project was completed—on time and on budget—he insisted on buying the Maleks out. There followed a tense and emotional meeting, the kind that is as likely to end up in a lawsuit as an agreement, throughout which Amir sat stone-faced and silent. When the shouting died down, Amir leaned over to Shahram and said, "Just tell him

this is our price." Shahram did so, and Schroeder paid it, leaving everyone to celebrate a successful outcome.

Looking back now, Gillespie says, "I'm a fan," adding that the
Maleks have always shown integrity in their business dealings and
"have never been anything but generous" in their personal relationship. They competed in other deals, but Gillespie says it was never a
negative. "If I lost a piece of property to them [in a bidding war], I
didn't mind," he says, adding, "I knew that the project was landing in
a good place."

One of the Maleks' next big projects was another shopping centre,
and one that turned out to be groundbreaking, not just physically but
also for its planning and design. The site, introduced to the Maleks by
a young agent named Chris Moradian, was in a part of South Surrey
that people are more inclined to identify as White Rock. It was a large
block on 152 Street, a suburban thoroughfare where strip malls had
become the standard of the day. Bankers and future tenants might
have expected more of the same: a wide swath of pavement with lots
of free parking and a series of walk-up storefronts, set well back. But
the planners at the City of Surrey were looking to establish a more
conventional commercial street front, with stores right up to the sidewalk and parking underground and in the rear. The property came
with a significant amount of additional density, including room for
second- and third-storey retail and office space, an innovation in the
area at the time. Other developers looked at the risk of this innovative—which is to say, unproven—form in a car-oriented suburb and
they kept walking. But the Maleks liked the site and the opportunity,
so Shahram and Reza Navabi, Marjan's husband who had recently
joined the company, started knocking on doors, looking to identify
prospective tenants who would make the project practical. Reza and
Shahram would meet at the local Muffin Break after driving from

the North Shore to plan the day's leasing strategy, and they became acquainted with a convivial Block Brothers realtor by the name of Ted Crosby, known as the "Sheriff of White Rock," who also helped them on the leasing side. They already had General Paint, which was the sort of business you might expect to find in a strip mall, so the key was to get commitments from businesses that could fill out the space and be relevant in a more urban street setting. Margarita's, an iconic fashion store, and Murchie's Tea were early and important successes. The Maleks also ran a design competition, through which they engaged Waisman Dewar Grout Carter Architects, with Stu Lyon as the architect in charge. (Stu would become one of Millennium's chief architects at the Olympic Village project almost twenty years later.) Since the family was doing the whole thing on spec, they were delighted to find funding from Standard Trust through their representative, a capable Scotsman named Alex Fox. He and a knowledgeable financial advisor by the name of Larry Lazzari, whom the Maleks had met at around the same time, were very kind and helpful, forging a career-long relationship and friendship.

The resulting Windsor Square, which Armeco built with its own construction team, was a speculative risk that became an undisputed success, a 2- to 3-storey full-block reinforced concrete development that wound up anchoring a planned high-street section along 152 Street. It also won an Award of Excellence in the Development of the Urban Environment in the next Urban Development Institute awards. Shahram says, "After the project was finished, and take-out financing was arranged through Standard Trust, the leasing agents Brent McRae and Steve Nichols approached us and said they had a buyer for the centre. It was Penreal, the Air Canada pension fund managers." Peter and Shahram were tempted, but they hesitated, thinking the family might like to keep the building as equity. But

Amir was delighted to take the money and move on to the next deal. He had bigger plans.

The Maleks' ability to recognize the value of projects that eluded other developers continued. The company's next major undertaking looked to some like the wrong building in the wrong place. Shahram had come across a corner parcel in a low-rise, low-density neighbourhood in Burnaby, on the corner of Beresford and Willingdon. There seemed little to recommend it, other than a brand-new Patterson SkyTrain station a block and a half away.

The inaugural stage of Metro Vancouver's light rapid transit SkyTrain had been built from downtown Vancouver through Burnaby to New Westminster just in time for the World Exposition on Transportation, Expo 86. Few developers had yet come to understand how much the line was destined to transform the region, changing development patterns and supercharging property values near the elevated guideway and, especially, near stations. So, while the competition dallied, Amir, who had seen in Europe the influence that rapid transit could have on nearby property, gave Shahram the go-ahead to put in an offer to buy it.

Amir sent Shahram to Citibank, hoping the New York lenders who had financed Regency Place would carry the deal in return for a share of the profits. Citibank agreed, and Carlton-on-the-Park, a 21-storey, 110-unit condo tower, proved this new model in a Metrotown neighbourhood that was about to boom. It was an enormous success, with local buyers snapping up all the condos before construction was completed. The family also used another of its own new firms, a construction company called Belmont, to build the development. Belmont was headed by Mohammad Sorkhou, manager of Armeh's road building, concrete, and asphalt plant division in Iran before the Revolution, and George Lockery, a smart, Cambridge-educated engineer who had previously worked for Stevenson Construction. And the Maleks repaid Citibank their loan in full together with a 30 percent share of the profits.

To understand how risky—how heretical—this development seemed at the time, it's critical to understand the dynamics of the Metro Vancouver region. As a coherent but distributed city, Vancouver is a bit like New York: people who don't live there think of each city as a single entity. Most out-of-towners envision the Manhattan skyline, paying scant attention to the outer boroughs and drawing little distinction between, say, Brooklyn and the Bronx. Similarly, in Vancouver, folks-from-away might think mostly about the part of the city that they see in tourist photos or Olympic television coverage. Vancouver's dense downtown peninsula tends to be the most picturesque part of the city, surrounded by ocean on three sides and edged, gloriously, by a steep range of mountains on the North Shore. But the greater Vancouver metropolitan region includes twenty-one separate municipalities and one self-governing Indigenous community, the Tsawwassen First Nation. Each of those communities has its own history and own character. Burnaby, for example, was once regarded as a working-class suburb, i.e, a lower-income, low-rise bedroom community where you expected to find service industries and single-family housing that was more affordable than homes in the higher-priced neighbourhoods of the City of Vancouver proper. In the late 1980s, there was no "downtown" Burnaby, no high-rise cluster that you'd see from a long way away.

So, when work began at Carlton-on-the-Park, in the low-rise Willingdon and Beresford neighbourhood, competitors shook their heads. The Maleks didn't look like early adopters; they looked like they were lost, building a tower among single-family homes and 3-storey walk-ups. Drive by that corner today, and Carlton-on-the-Park sits unobtrusively on the leading edge of a forest of towers in the second-most prominent urban neighbourhood in the region, after the West End in Vancouver. The Maleks were at the front of what would become a very popular and successful parade.

A subsequent opportunity required even more far-sighted perspective—and a shockingly expensive plane ticket. In early 1990, Steve Nichols, one of the principals who had negotiated the Windsor Square sale, phoned to say that he had a line on an urgent and exciting development opportunity in the collapsing but newly accessible Soviet Union. In May, with Mikhail Gorbachev in the Kremlin and the spirit of *glasnost* in the air, Shahram found himself holed up in a huge suite in a downtown Moscow Warsaw Pact hotel. It was the kind of place where Muscovites welcomed Western visitors who were bold enough to peek behind the Iron Curtain, and it was a classic of its time: big and cold, with Soviet pretensions of luxury, but threadbare towels. Shahram remembers spending an uneasy night, not because he was afraid to be in Russia, but because his half-empty hostelry was stark and lonely—and because he wasn't quite sure what he was doing there.

Nichols had described a "once-in-a-lifetime" opportunity in Moscow. He had asked Shahram to make the journey to Russia to take a look. The brothers were skeptical. They were just getting settled in the Vancouver development world; it would seem something of an overreach to start planning a Russian operation as well. But Nichols had been persistent, arguing—accurately—that with the Soviet Union just beginning to open up to foreign investment, this might be a chance to get in on the ground floor. Shahram finally relented, flying to London, then Stockholm, and finally to Moscow, to be greeted by their Russian contact. Shahram recalls first names only: Genady, who met him at the airport, and Valery and Igor, who hosted a lavish dinner at the hotel's rooftop restaurant before seeing Shahram to his room.

These details, while sparse, are carefully recorded in one of the daily journals that Shahram keeps. He says, "My dad always said, 'Write everything down.'" Amir expected his sons to make a record of what was happening today and set out the program for what they planned to do tomorrow. Shahram has a reliable record running back to his earliest days in the development business. The notes are neither extensive nor fussy. There are no long essays, scrawled over many pages. Rather, the entries are short, purposeful memos-to-self, inked quickly into small, elegant notebooks.

Shahram can say with confidence that, on the morning of May 21, 1990, Igor picked him up after breakfast and took him to the outskirts of Moscow, to a vast piece of property which, until recently, had been in the hands of the Soviet Ministry of Defence. The land had been selected as the future headquarters of *Glavkosmos*, a partially privatized subsidiary of the Russian state space corporation *Roscosmos*. The opportunity was both unique and potentially huge. Or perhaps not. Shahram says that his Soviet hosts merely showed him the site and said, "Here is the land. What do you want to do?" There was no plan, no "owner" in any conventional sense—no limits, but no structure. There was, for example, nothing so banal as an established zoning. Shahram soon found he was more interested in an exit strategy than an investment.

He enjoyed a couple more days in this historic, transitioning city— with dinner in the luxurious Savoy Hotel and an evening of symphony and opera around the corner at the Bolshoi Theatre. The Russians were incredibly gracious and there were things they did extraordinarily well, even while their political system and economy were crumbling in the final days of the Cold War.

In hindsight, the agents who had introduced the Air Canada pension fund were right about the promising future of Glavkosmos: it has thrived in the decades since. Today, the company sells everything from satellites to launch services. If you have Jeff Bezos–level disposable income, Glavkosmos can put you on a Soyuz-2 rocket and send you to the International Space Station. If you're on a budget, the company website advertises "the first official Russian space merch"—everything from fridge magnets to T-shirts with cartoon images of busty kosmonauts in skin-tight space suits.

Shahram wastes no time thinking about the road not taken. Looking back on the Moscow trip, he says, "I'm glad to have gone. It was another one of those once-in-a-lifetime experiences," But he's equally glad to have waived off any further Russian adventure.

Back in Metro Vancouver, in the shadow of the SkyTrain guideway, the Maleks found another piece of property that no one else seemed to want. It was a 6.5-hectare industrial property, the site of a Domglas Inc. warehouse, three subway stops beyond Carlton-on-the-Park, in a Burnaby district called Edmonds. Here, where there was really nothing other than a new SkyTrain station, the Maleks were thinking big—as many as seven condo towers that, together, would comprise a complete new neighbourhood. In the words of Michael Geller, an architect, developer, and planner-about-town who has known the brothers since the early 1980s and admires their work, "This was not just a series of buildings, but a real community."

"When we first saw the property, at the suggestion of Peter Wardle, the architect who owned it at the time, we couldn't believe our eyes," Shahram says. "There was this Skytrain station virtually sitting on the site, surrounded by low-rise industrial buildings, and bordered by Byrne Creek Park to the West. It was the epitome of the ideal property our father had told us to look for. But it was bigger than anything we had done in Vancouver."

The Maleks met Wardle to get a sense of his ambitions for the property and then they walked the 16 acres with their university friend, architect Fred Adab, and asked him what he thought and whether he could think of anyone who might want to join the venture. Adab loved the property and linked the brothers to Hassan Khosrowshahi of the Future Shop group, a respected businessman who stayed on as a partner through the first two towers.

After acquiring the property, the Maleks telegraphed their seriousness by hiring Arthur Erickson, at the time arguably the biggest name in Canadian architecture, to work on the master plan. They also engaged talented architect Larry Doyle of Hamilton Doyle Architects, who, with partner Gerald Hamilton, they knew well from their work on the Maleks' first two major developments, Regency Place and Carlton-on-the-Park. Gerald had been courteous and kind and had embraced the Maleks as newcomers when they were first starting in Vancouver. Larry was meticulous in his incorporation of the structural aspects of buildings at the beginning of the planning process and is reputed among developers as one of the most efficient in his field.

The Maleks drove with Arthur from downtown Vancouver to the Burnaby site, and they recall how gracious he was. "Arthur talked with a smile about when he had met the Shah and Queen Farah of Iran in Tehran and about his work in Saudi Arabia, and he said that he would be happy to work with us. He was modest and kind, something that we had not expected from such a famous architect," Shahram says.

The Maleks then set about negotiating with the City of Burnaby, which they describe as "very open but very height-conscious at the time." This was an industrial site. There were few residents in the area who might object to towers. But even so, while Burnaby planners encouraged residential development near the SkyTrain, they seemed skittish at the proposal of something above the 13- to 14-storey range. Peter then leaned in, suggesting that a few more storeys might make the project more viable. When Burnaby head planner Ken Ito asked how many storeys they had in mind, Shahram says that Peter blurted out: "twenty-eight." They both say now that it was a number straight off the top of his head; there'd been no discussion about it before-hand. And yet, to everyone's surprise, Ito carried the idea forward and Burnaby city council said yes.

A greater surprise, perhaps, came in a sticky negotiation over the inclusion of a large formal garden. At Shahram's urging, architect Larry Doyle and landscape architect John Lantzius had designed a grand central space that would serve and unify the whole neighbourhood. It was not quite the 800-hectare gardens of Versailles, but it was inspired by the elegant gardens that the Maleks had grown to love in the UK, as well as in France. The City of Burnaby's reaction was quick and sharp: the brothers recall one of the Burnaby planners saying the designs were "too imperial." The planners wanted each tower to have its own swimming pool and landscaping, which they thought would be less complicated than having six or seven different strata corporations all sharing responsibility for this grand, central space. But the Maleks were committed to their vision. They held their ground, and the City relented. The garden is beloved in the neighbourhood and admired farther afield. Pick any sunny Saturday in the season and you can wander among the flowers or watch a parade of brides and grooms taking advantage of the neighbour-hood's best backdrop for wedding photos.

The final hurdle, the ultimate obstacle, was financing. The Maleks had already concluded two very successful projects with financing from Citibank: Regency Place and Carlton-on-the-Park. So, you might think, as they did, that the lender would be game for a new adventure. Shahram shakes his head at the thought. "Their lead person had lived in the Burnaby neighbourhood of Edmonds, and he hated it—he called it 'rat infested!'" And he turned them down flat. They finally found local financing from Belzberg & Co., and they built the award-winning, 26-storey Savoy Carlton on spec, selling it slowly to an initially skeptical public but ultimately so successfully that the Bank of Montreal was eager to step in and finance the 30-storey Belgravia, the tower that came next.

Development is a risky business under most circumstances, but it's particularly risky to build on spec. In the Vancouver real estate market today, you have to find a promising piece of land and usually also secure a first round of financing, as property values have made outright purchase daunting. That large loan racks up interest charges while you move through what can be years of planning and rezoning. Once a residential project is approved, you then have to pre-sell 60 to 70 percent of the units before you can convince a lender to advance the next, large round of financing for construction.

Even in the early 1990s, it was bold to go into Edmonds with an imaginative master plan, a high-end product, and no buyers already committed. This kind of development was still innovative in Metro Vancouver, and even today, few people have the vision—or the patience—to buy a luxury condo overlooking an abandoned bottling plant on the promise that, some day in the middling future, there will be a "too imperial" garden, where they will be able to wander in sophisticated meditation or luxuriate in the sun over a good book. Nevertheless, the Maleks built—and sold—the Savoy Carlton in 1991 and the second tower, the Belgravia, in 1996. By the time the Maleks were starting on the third tower, Claridges, Shahram and Peter were optimistic they could find a reasonable pre-sale market. And they were able to convince the emerging "condo king" Bob Rennie and his then-partner Dan Ulinder to venture out from their home base in Vancouver into the wilds of Burnaby.

Bob Rennie is an undisputed marketing leader in the hot Metro Vancouver region; his company does hundreds of millions of dollars in real estate deals every year. Rennie Project Marketing Corporation has 92 employees and 160 brokers, and few developers even *think* about starting a new project without checking in with Rennie on every detail from location to suite design. Bob knows what sells. "It's all in the data," he says. "I have three demographers and three economists on staff. It's what we do."

In the early 1990s, Rennie and Ulinder were still experimenting with condo pre-sales and, in Peter's words, they were "downtown people" who had worked mostly on projects in the densest parts of the City of Vancouver. Still, Shahram adds, "they were like magicians" in the selling of condos, finding buyers and creating the buzz. It seemed worth it to coax them to take on a project in Burnaby.

For his part, Rennie credits the Maleks not just for the success of the Claridges building in the Edmonds City-in-the-Park project but also for helping to develop the still-nascent Rennie sales machine. As a self-described "fluke of nature in the real estate industry," Rennie notes that he never finished high school, but he says that "every building I did with [the Maleks] was a university course." He says, "They have such vision. Their family has been monumental in my career."

About the Edmonds location, Rennie adds, "They *saw* transit. They understood, from their European background, that transit drives density." The notion of transit-oriented density is now garden-variety obvious in Vancouver, as it is in most other urban markets. Developers squabble ferociously for any piece of property near a major transit stop and, especially, near a rapid transit station. They know that buyers love the convenience. But in the early 1990s, these locations still seemed out of the way and out of mind. Again, the Maleks were early to the party.

Rennie says the brothers also understood what it would take to "turn East Burnaby into Central Burnaby." When Millennium arrived, Rennie says, the Edmonds neighbourhood was "a waste, a garbage dump." But the Maleks proved themselves to be big-picture thinkers, first by including in the project the garden that Rennie calls "the mews." ("It's very British to have this formal park.") They also developed a quaint grocery, which, in addition to providing a very practical service, added the kind of texture that turns a housing development into a community.

There is another interesting French element to the design, the now widely disparaged notion of "towers in a park." Conceived by the Swiss-French architect Le Corbusier early in the twentieth century, the name perfectly describes the theme: towers, spaced about relatively evenly in a park. Unfortunately, the form was reinterpreted by builders of cheap public housing everywhere from London to New York City: the towers were ugly; the parks too small, poorly tended—or paved!—and ultimately dangerous. In those iterations, people hate the resulting neighbourhoods and urban revisionists have taken great pleasure in the last forty or fifty years in knocking the towers down. The Maleks, however, found a way to do Le Corbusier proud, so much so that when the City of Burnaby started insisting upon a low-rise townhouse component on one side of the park, the residents from previous towers in the development revolted, insisting that the tower form prevail. As it does today, to wide acclaim.

The word that Rennie comes back to most often when describing both Millennium and the brothers is "civility." He asks, rhetorically and, given his position as someone whose business depends heavily on the development industry, indiscreetly: "How many developers are gentlemen?" The business is famous for its hardbitten dealmakers, people who are often more comfortable in snarling work-site battles with belligerent subcontractors than they are doing deals in wood-panelled boardrooms. Peter and Shahram, on the other hand, are unfailingly courtly, in every venue. "They love to make money," Rennie says, "but they never come off the integrity square."

According to Rennie, Millennium buildings have a similar ethos, and improve property values around their location. "They give the neighbourhood a civility to grow into." While other developers are driving inexorably to the bottom line, stripping away anything that isn't absolutely essential, Rennie says that the Maleks are just as likely to wrap a social housing project in limestone, as the Maleks have done—investing in lasting value when another developer might more likely have gone cheap.

Millennium has also largely resisted the temptation of what has come to be known as "starchitecture," which describes a situation where a local developer hires a hot, international architectural luminary who gifts the city a building that, in Rennie's characterization, sticks out like "a dandy in a floppy purple hat." Peter says that Millennium's philosophy of architecture is clear: "Sometimes it's the exterior of the buildings that architects think about, not the interior. But we are very careful in our buildings because people actually have to live in them. They are not monuments."

Certainly, Millennium has worked with star architects. Some, like Stu Lyon of GBL Architects, earned their stardom partly based on buildings that the Maleks commissioned. They also commissioned plans and buildings by local stars who already had an international reputation, like Arthur Erickson, and by international stars the Maleks courted for their vision and style.

Principal in the latter category is Robert A.M. Stern, the former Yale School of Architecture dean whose 265-person New York firm, Robert A.M. Stern Architects, LLP, has, in the past fifty years, written the book on classical elegance. While Stern's team has done some playfully modern work, like the Disney Ambassador Hotel in

Urayasu-shi, the first Disney-branded hotel in Japan, his portfolio is filled with buildings that are formal and stately, whether they are soaring residential towers off Central Park or brick-and-stone Ivy League colleges or libraries.

When the Maleks started talking about Stern, their brother-in-law Essie Djafarian, a UK-trained architect and businessman who is married to their middle sister, Maryam, jumped in as an enthusiastic facilitator, contacting Stern's office and smoothing out the details. Shahram and Peter both say Stern was a pleasure to deal with and an immense talent. Shahram says that one of Stern's associates had warned them in advance that Stern was, "Woody Allen–like, so don't worry if he complains a lot." It was a jesting reference, but proved out, as Stern amusingly found fault in everything from the weather to the weight of the cutlery that they used during their first lunch. The Maleks had invited him to town to design a building for a prime property they had assembled on Bellevue Avenue, a waterfront street in West Vancouver that was distinguished, at the time, by a row of apartment blocks whose principal architectural accomplishment was to block the view. True to form, when Stern saw the street, he said, "I like to work within the context of other buildings, but those buildings are awful."

From that point forward however, he was both resolutely positive and endlessly accommodating. When Shahram mentioned that the brothers had admired Stern's design of the Brooklyn Law School, Stern said "great" and immediately started sketching at the table between his underweight knife and fork. By the end of lunch, he had cast the first renderings of the building that would become Edgewater—a slim, 15-storey tower with twelve full-floor apartments, including a two-level penthouse, and three townhomes in the base. Externally, it has the stolid grace of an Upper East Side co-op—the kind of place where you're not allowed to buy an apartment unless you can convince your neighbours that you are (as Rennie might put it) *civil* as well as rich. When the Maleks took the project to the District of West Vancouver for the first time, the design panel rejected it by a vote of seven to zero, saying that the design wasn't "West Coast enough." The Maleks suspected that the panelists felt snubbed; Stern had been double-booked and couldn't appear for the review, leaving the West Van reviewers to think he was taking too much for granted.

The Maleks booked a second review at a time when Stern was available to make the case for his design, and the design panel gave a thumbs-up, this time by a vote of seven to zero in favour of the project. And no wonder. While it's true that Edgewater doesn't look like any of the sterile glass towers that have come to exemplify a lot of recent West Coast architecture, the form is elegantly tall and thin, minimizing the view blockage while giving uphill neighbours something new to see and admire. The interiors are glorious, with classical pilasters, inlaid marble floors, 10-foot ceilings and—in every suite—the best waterfront *and* mountain views in the city. The 3,350-square-foot apartments sold in 1997 for $1.5 million, which Bob Rennie now complains was, practically speaking, "free." At the time, he says, "you couldn't buy a fifty-foot lot [in West Vancouver] for $1.5 million that would allow you to build that much density." Rennie says he still regrets that he didn't buy one of the suites himself.

The next project the Maleks did with Stern was also in West Vancouver, and was more controversial. The site was at 540 Clyde Avenue, a gorgeous spot up against the Capilano River. Since 1957, it had been the home of the Park Royal Hotel. A rumpled institution with the bar, garden, and pretensions of an old English inn, the Park Royal was much loved in the larger community—but mostly ignored. It was easy enough to generate a crowd of people who wanted it preserved, but business owners need customers with money, not crowds with a romantic attachment to an empty hotel. There was public grumbling after the owners invited Millennium to create a new development scheme. But most critics revised their opinion when they saw Stern's design emerge on the riverbank. The four concrete mid-rises, two gracefully curved toward the Capilano River, now frame a street that looks like it could be an upscale residential neighbourhood in the best parts of Paris or Copenhagen. There are seventy-nine suites and sixteen rentals in a coherent and elegant cluster. As the first thing you now see coming off the Lions Gate Bridge, the development has redefined the front door to West Vancouver.

Throughout this period, Millennium was also maintaining its profile—and its good reputation—in the City of Vancouver. One of their most unusual projects was another that made competitors think that the Malek brothers had lost their minds. This was on Hastings Street, in Vancouver's Downtown Eastside, too often identified as "the poorest postal code in Canada." It's a neighbourhood that brings shame on the City of Vancouver, filled with people who are destitute and desperate, while just a ten-minute walk from some of the most beautiful and expensive real estate in the country.

A century ago, this was the very heart of the city, and there is still a collection of beautiful old buildings that speak eloquently of lost prosperity. One such treasure is The Province Building, a 7-storey Edwardian that, when it was built in 1908–09, must have seemed like a skyscraper. (When the 17-storey Sun Tower was built around the corner three years later, it was heralded as the tallest building in the Commonwealth.) The Province Building was originally home to the *News-Advertiser* and to the Vancouver branch of the Eastern Townships Bank (now CIBC), but it was purchased in 1924 by *The Daily Province*, and expanded with a broad, second-storey bridge over the alley to the Edgett Building where *The Province* had its presses.

In subsequent decades, the building's fortunes followed those of the neighbourhood until, in the late 1990s, it was a rundown hulk with a "For Lease" sign in the window. Driving by one day on his way to Burnaby to visit City-in-the-Park, Shahram was struck by the block's beauty, its evident strength, and its potential, and he immediately picked up the car phone to ask Prospero Realty (listed as the leasing agents) if the building might be for sale. To his surprise, they said it could be. There followed what must be the worst-ever property negotiation. The Maleks learned that the building had just changed hands, and that the new owner was "a potential flipper," who bought and sold buildings sometimes without any real plan to manage or renew. When they reached him through the leasing agents, he said, yes, he might consider an offer of $2 million. Peter says, "We said, 'How about $1.8?' and he came back and said, 'How about $2.2?'" Committed, they paid the $2.2 million, which the Maleks still regarded as a steal, and Peter is forever on the lookout for an opportunity to negotiate another deal in the same way—this time in Millennium's favour.

The building was a wreck. The marble columns had been painted pink and someone had installed drop ceilings that covered up the original mouldings and plasterwork that distinguished upscale banks of the day. They had also defaced the whole scene with the later addition of machinery hooks for industrial winches. Peter says, "Pulling it all apart was like an archeological expedition." The brothers contacted CIBC, which still had archival photos of the Eastern Townships Bank, and they used them as a guide to restore the building to its original grandeur.

All the while, Peter says, "people were saying, 'Why would you buy such a thing?'"—a question that became even more pressing when Millennium finished the project and moved their own offices from the Bentall Centre—at the time one of the most desirable office locations in the city—to The Province Building, across the street from Victory

Square, a park best known as a gathering place for drug dealers. But the offices were beautiful—and they were just across the street, in the other direction, from the old Woodward's store. Its redevelopment in 2010 lifted property values and turned out to be a redefining moment for the whole neighbourhood, most notably by adding a huge addition to the downtown campus of Simon Fraser University.

Millennium bid on the Woodward's project as well. While their proposal didn't win, it left a lasting and positive impression on City of Vancouver planners. The old Woodward's department store, the first section of which dated to 1903, was for many decades the gravitational centre of Vancouver's downtown commercial district. The store flourished well into the 1960s, when the city's commercial centre began migrating west toward Granville Street. By 1993, Woodward's was bankrupt and the store closed. But the building was still iconic, an emotional anchor even as the immediate neighbourhood had drifted into decline. The prospect of redevelopment became intensely political and an early proposal to replace it with a gentrifying housing development crashed badly. Neighbourhood activists demanded that any redevelopment should support the local population and include a large portion of social housing. In the early 2000s, the City of Vancouver took ownership of the property and put out a call for proposals. There were three bidders: Ian Gillespie's Westbank; a consortium including the Holborn Group and Concert Properties; and Millennium. Millennium was the lesser-known player to City staff, and the Maleks showed up with the richest bid and the most ambitious plan. While their competitors had bound themselves quite closely to the City's 70-foot (5- to 7-storey) height limit, Millennium had looked at the economics of the project and decided it required something much bigger, so they included in their proposal a tower of more than 300 feet. They also suggested a gesture that some Downtown Eastside activists—and some City staff—decried as an offence to the neighbourhood's history. One of the most iconic elements of the Woodward's location was a huge "W"—a de facto corporate logo—that had towered over the store on top of a 25-metre replica of the Eiffel Tower since 1944. Peter and Shahram suggested the W should be brought down, preserved, and placed at ground level as an enduring piece of public art.

Chuck Brook, who had been working with Millennium as a real estate planning consultant and who was part of the presentation to City staff, says, "They practically threw us out of the room." Brook says that the late city councillor and one-time Downtown Eastside housing activist Jim Green, who was effectively leading the project on the City's behalf, was particularly offended, saying that a tower would be an unforgivable blot on the low-rise skyline of the immediate neighbourhood and of historic Gastown to the north. In addition, Green said, there was no way that W would ever be brought to ground.

Millennium wasn't brought into subsequent negotiations, and Westbank wound up with the commission, which ultimately included two towers over 30 storeys. Westbank also built a new W on top of a new faux Eiffel Tower, and—exactly reflecting Millennium's proposal—it brought the original W to a ground-level courtyard, where it sits as an enduring piece of public art.

A last example of a project that cemented Millennium's good name at Vancouver City Hall was a mixed-use building that was proposed for a city-owned parking lot on Robson and Richards streets. Today, the location seems very much part of downtown, but in 2004, when they first began looking at the deal, Richards was a busy, noisy, four-lane traffic thoroughfare offering few temptations to stop and none at all to stroll. That part of Robson was devoid of pedestrian activity. The Maleks offered the City close to $100 per buildable square foot—which the brothers say was dismissed as "a crazy price at the time"—and they turned heads once more. You could buy land for far less, even near the central part of downtown.

But the Maleks could do the math. They knew that the key to making money at this price point was going to have to come in the mix of uses. The property was zoned to accommodate residential, office, and commercial space, but the lot was too near the central business district for the City to allow a purely residential tower. At the same time, it was a little out of the way for Triple-A office space and not quite big enough to create the floor plates that would attract a major retailer. Millennium solved the first part of the problem by choosing to build a hotel, which was allowed within the commercial zoning. It's the site today of L'Hermitage, a luxury sixty-suite boutique hotel, run by younger sister Ellie Malek, that attracts the kind of discerning clientele who are looking for more quality and less profile. They solved the second problem by buying the property immediately to the north. That opened up sufficient room to build second-storey commercial space where there is now a HomeSense over a first-storey IGA grocery store, the kind of neighbourhood-friendly service and convenience that is highly valued in Vancouver's heavily residential downtown.

Still, there wasn't enough space. The location is one of the densest parts of downtown. For every extra condo you might add in the residential tower above the hotel, you need room to park more cars in the floors below. This, too, was solvable. There was a rundown, single-room-occupancy (SRO) hotel still further to the north, closer to West Georgia—the kind of property that is always for sale, for a price. But it was complicated. Like many modern major cities, Vancouver has an intractable problem with homelessness and these beat-up old hotels, while sometimes obnoxious and barely safe, still offer affordable shelter, which is vanishingly rare. Accordingly, the City of Vancouver has imposed stringent conditions on developers who are looking to buy and gentrify—who would knock down low-income homes and replace them with condos so pricy that even young professionals are stretched by the tariff. While discussing options with City planners, the Maleks found themselves, suddenly and unhappily, in the news. The still-influential Councillor Jim Green was on the radio, complaining about the presumed loss of more SRO hotel rooms that, at this point, could be demolished on condition the developer pay a fee to the city. Again, solvable. Green himself called Shahram to say that a deal was possible, but only if Millennium was willing to replace the SRO rooms with an equal number of non-market housing units. Millennium agreed, creating a Vancouver model. It was the first such deal in Vancouver and became a model for future developments.

In the minds of most developers in most markets, such a proposal might have been a non-starter. The Maleks were drafting plans for an exclusive hotel at the base of a luxury condo tower. There was reason to be concerned that high-end hotel guests and well-heeled condo buyers would have reservations about sharing their building envelope—and sidewalk space—with the candidates for social housing. The usual solution to that problem has also grown controversial. Social activists object to the presence of a so-called poor door in mixed social-market housing developments—a second-rate entrance, usually hidden in an out-of-the-way spot, through which social-housing residents must pass so the wealthy guests and neighbours don't have to watch them coming and going. But the brothers had a solution that was more elegant—and more generous. They built forty-six non-market housing units, many *more* than had been in the old SRO hotel. And they built them in an elegant continuance of the L'Hermitage structure. The lobby and front door of the social housing block are in keeping with the high-value theme. There is no concierge, but otherwise, the entryway looks just as daunting and unaffordable as any other downtown Vancouver condo tower.

These are only a few examples of the projects Millennium completed in their first few decades, but they are representative of the variety and consistent quality of their work. The Maleks were unafraid of risk and, often, undaunted when the price of something seemed high, as long as the numbers worked. They were resourceful, innovative, and creative, and they proved, time and again, that an extra investment in quality paid a dividend. In the highly competitive and often bruising development world, they were variously liked or admired—but in all cases they were trusted. Theirs was the company you called when you had a project that was interesting, difficult, urgent, and demanding.

So, when Jody Andrews from the City of Vancouver phoned Shahram in the summer of 2005, they weren't surprised. They weren't even particularly flattered. Rather, they were curious and skeptical. Andrews, the deputy city manager and project manager for the 2010 Winter Olympics, was soliciting their interest as potential bidders on a new kind of Olympic dream. And if such an opportunity was pregnant with risk? Well, great opportunities always are.

THE OLYMPIC CHALLENGE

"The biggest sin is fear. The biggest recreation is work."

These were the precepts by which Amir Malek lived his life—and they are the lessons he left for his children. Mahin Malek, Amir's wife for seventy-two years, says now: "For Amir, nothing was impossible. He used to say, 'Put me in the wilderness with nothing, and I will still thrive.'" And thrive he did, establishing business empires in three countries—Iran, France, and Canada—on three continents. He also set a high bar for his sons, who adored their father, and still embrace the "recreation" of work in the course of extending his legacy.

The chance to build on that legacy arose in 2005, when the City of Vancouver tried to draw the Maleks in on a project to build an Olympic Village on 80 acres of poisoned industrial land on Vancouver's Southeast False Creek. Amir had already built an Olympic venue once—even if it was never used for that event. So, a new challenge—the call to build a new Olympic Village for the 2010 Winter Games in

Vancouver—might have looked a little like destiny, even if they didn't initially think of it that way.

"What appealed to us was, like City-in-the-Park, the ability to build a brand-new community in Vancouver from scratch. And we knew we had both the local and international experience to do the job," Shahram says.

The potential was fantastic—although you needed vision to see it. Given the world-renowned urban treasure it is today, it's hard to imagine False Creek as the fetid backwater it once was. It might serve to step back even further to when this small inlet terminated in a vast and muddy tidal flat, likely the site of a seasonal banquet for the Indigenous Peoples who lived in the region and harvested its bounty for millennia before the arrival of the first colonial settlers. The "creek" was declared false in 1867, when English sea captain George Richards first charted its banks. Rather than a freshwater tributary, Capt. Richards found only a salty slough that ran north through what is now Chinatown and Gastown to connect with Burrard Inlet. Then came generations of "improvements." The Royal Engineers filled in the swampy bits to connect the Vancouver peninsula to land further east, and the early industrialists set about building sawmills, shipyards, rail yards, foundries, metalworks, and a huge salt refinery—all operating with increasing intensity and paying little attention to how much pollution was spilling onto the land and into the water. Well into the 1970s, the creek was a malodorous home for heavy industry, with sawmill beehive burners belching so much smoke that it hung in a near-permanent fog over the Cambie Street Bridge. Granville Island and the southwest part of False Creek got a makeover in the 1970s with a city-led, federally funded renewal and housing project that was hotly controversial at the time. There were critics aplenty who predicted that no one would ever want to live in waterfront homes on a smelly inlet, facing a noisy industrial north shore. They were proved wrong—but slowly.

Then came Expo 86—not a full-blown World Expo (as accredited by the Paris-based Bureau International des Expositions) but a smaller-scale World Exposition on Transportation. While the Expo fit the technical description of the second-tier event, no one told anyone in Vancouver—or the 22 million people who stepped through the gate—that this was supposed to be a smaller party. The burst of energy and the bright lights of world attention launched Vancouver as a global destination of choice for real estate investors as well as for tourists. With the provincial government taking the lead, the forces of redevelopment chased off the heavy industries and assembled 173 acres along the north shore, most of it purchased in 1988 by the Hong Kong business mogul Li Ka-shing. The nature and quality of planning and development that occurred in the next thirty years, as Li's successor company Concord Pacific developed the site, transformed False Creek. It also cemented Vancouver's reputation as a global model for the design and construction of buildings and neighbourhoods that proved a dense urban environment could be livable and attractive, not just for single twenty-somethings but also for families who were once destined to head for the suburbs.

After all that work, there remained a huge brownfield on the southeast shore of False Creek, a swath of abandoned and under-utilized industrial land, including the 80-acre parcel that would become the site for the Olympic Village. The City of Vancouver was clearly enthused about the potential for this site. As early as 1991, while Concord Pacific was moving into full swing developing the north side of False Creek, Vancouver City Council proclaimed Southeast False Creek as the future home of a model sustainable community, and by 1993, the City was buying up major pieces of property. The

first person to propose those purchases was Sam Sullivan, a city councillor who later ascended to the mayoralty, where he served from 2005
to 2008. Sullivan looks back on that iteration of Southeast False Creek
as "a centre for old-style industry, with greasy, dirty buildings with
metal sides and roofs. It was all dark and dingy and loud. There were
all these screaming machines." This, Sullivan speculates, is where
Vancouver earned its nickname, "The Big Smoke." He says, "My dad
talked about the old fogs that were so bad you had to climb up tele-
phone poles to read the street names."

In 1999, the City began defining its ambitions more clearly, inviting
development that would achieve a new global standard of energy and
water efficiency, and general environmental sustainability—regularly
surpassing previous code requirements by as much as 20 or 30 percent.
But not much actually happened. With Concord Pacific still building
out its property on the north shore, the real estate market was flush
with new product and there was no other trigger to begin a large competing development so nearby.

That began to change in 2002, when, in support of its 2010
Olympics bid, the City signed a multi-party agreement with the
Vancouver Organizing Committee (VANOC), promising to build an
athletes' village that could house nearly three thousand competitors
in return for a $30-million Olympic contribution. This undertaking
provided an inspiration for how the City would use the land—and
a deadline for when. The whole prospect went from aspirational
to fully intentional in June 2003, when the International Olympic
Committee confirmed Vancouver as the winning bidder.

With the clock ticking, the City spent the next couple of years con-
sidering and enacting an Official Development Plan that set out urban
design guidelines and sustainability principles for the new neighbourhood. Numerous groups that wanted something from the City lined

up with their own requests, including for low-income and rental housing, a continuation of the seawall and other shoreline features, child-care centres, a community centre, abundant park and public spaces, and, again and again, the highest environmental standards yet established in a Vancouver neighbourhood.

All this seemed perfectly possible. The tower-and-podium model of development conceived and perfected in the Concord Pacific lands and across the downtown peninsula in Coal Harbour had come to symbolize the celebrated planning style that is now known as "Vancouverism." The form is a brilliant solution to dense urban design. Tower-and-podium buildings rest on a broad, low-rise base that provides a strong urban streetwall, defining and embracing adjacent streets and spaces. Above the podium rises a tall thin tower that is set back to avoid overwhelming the street or shrouding it in dark and permanent shadow. Thus, rather than the cramped, monolithic high-rise developments that have created the cold, dark canyons in the downtowns of New York or Seattle, Vancouver's newest neighbourhoods featured these tall thin forms—set back and nicely spaced so they provide high levels of urban density without completely blocking the sun or (crucial in Vancouver) obscuring the view. In the 166 acres of Concord Pacific lands that had already been developed, that built form had delivered a density of fifty-five units per acre, housing a population of thirteen thousand people—a standard similar to Liberty Village or Yonge-and-Eglinton in Toronto—and including 42 acres of public parkland. That's 200 square feet of park for every residential unit, which is one reason the north shore of False Creek has come to contain some of the most sought-after urban residential property in the world.

If you were thinking about developing something profitable and popular on the south shore, you already had a building form and a planning style that was not just publicly acceptable, but renowned.

By the early 2000s, there were likely a dozen or more planners, consultants, architects, and developers working the world circuit—from Abu Dhabi in the United Arab Emirates to Melbourne, Australia—as progenitors of Vancouverism, advocating everything from increased public consultation to the use of tower-and-podium buildings. Everyone was looking to copy Vancouver's success. If the task was to create housing for three thousand athletes that could be repurposed afterward as the residential soul of a new and beautiful neighbourhood, all you needed was five or six tower-and-podium high-rises: high-value residential condos above, mixed-use commercial and institutional podiums at street level, and lots of room left for parks. Easy.

Or not. Because, by this time, Vancouverites had moved beyond the point of accepting easy solutions. Scot Hein, then the senior urban designer at the City of Vancouver, says this was partly because "the sustainability gauntlet had been thrown down." Vancouver is the historical and emotional home of Greenpeace, and the City of Vancouver wears its environmentally conscious mantle proudly. Even beyond the question of achieving a high level of sustainability, the City knew that this neighbourhood was going to be an international focal point. Hein says, "We wanted to show a community that would be the best in the world when the cameras started rolling in 2010."

There was also something more—a level of architectural and planning ambition that went beyond preening for an international audience. Vancouverites had come to take themselves seriously as leaders in urban design, so the stakes of every new development seemed higher than the one before. In the course of redeveloping the north shore of False Creek, as well as the former rail-yard lands by Coal Harbour on Burrard Inlet, the City of Vancouver had developed three new communities of competence. First, the City had forged a planning department and a larger planning community that was both uniquely aspirational and increasingly savvy. For thirty years, the City of Vancouver's planners had been negotiating—and co-operating—on two of the biggest downtown brownfield redevelopments in North America: Concord Pacific's Expo lands on False Creek and the abandoned rail yards that Marathon Realty was developing on Coal Harbour.

Led by planning directors Larry Beasley and Anne McAfee, and supported by a shrewd real estate department, the City of Vancouver had learned how to extract its share of the profit when land was being rezoned from low-value industrial to extremely high-value commercial and residential. Recognizing the high costs of building urban infrastructure and filling in public amenities in these dense new developments, the City's bureaucrats learned to calculate the "uplift"—the increase in land value that came with the rezoning—and to extract a portion of that windfall. In effect, the city would say: right, if we rezone your property to allow for a higher use, the value will, say, double overnight, so we want half that increase to be spent on city infrastructure for the benefit of the people who are going to live in the new neighbourhood, and for the city as a whole. Vancouver's planners and its politicians learned how hard they could push—and they pushed hard. If you want evidence of how aggressive and successful Vancouver had become in this regard, you could compare the extensive community amenities on the Concord Pacific lands in Vancouver to the comparatively unambitious community contributions on the CN lands that Concord Pacific redeveloped in Toronto during the same period. The sixty-six currently developed acres on the Vancouver lands feature three parks that add up to more than 22 acres of space. The 40-odd-acre Concord CityPlace in Toronto boasts Canoe Landing Park, at 8 acres. Same developer: different result.

A second new community of competence had emerged among Vancouver's architects and private-sector urban designers. While a few starchitects have passed through the city over the years, much of Vancouver's good reputation for urban design (if not for glitzy buildings) can be traced to locals who made the best of these big, brownfield opportunities. Among these leaders and practitioners was a blue-ribbon group of nine who stepped up at a critical time to demand that new development on Southeast False Creek should be different from its nearby predecessors. In a public letter to the Vancouver mayor and council, they said, "We believe that a predominantly high-rise approach is the wrong point of departure for SEFC (Southeast False Creek)." This was an interesting—and influential—point of resistance, in part because of the identity of the nine signatories. Architect James Cheng, for example, is often credited with conceiving the tower-and-podium design. And his fellow architects Nigel Baldwin and James Hancock can also claim credit for a veritable forest of elegant high-rises now improving Vancouver's skyline. Peter Busby is renowned for raising the standards of sustainability. Joyce Drohan, Norm Hotson, and James Cheng, again, are regarded as being among the best urban designers of their generation, in demand in Vancouver and, increasingly, farther afield. Michael Geller had been the brash young planner who, on behalf of the Canada Mortgage and Housing Corporation, had taken the lead in southwest False Creek, the original development around Granville Island, and had gone on to serve as development manager for the Bayshore redevelopment, adjacent to Coal Harbour. That project, like Concord Pacific, is also an acknowledged triumph in making the most of the tower-and-podium form. Rounding out the group was Chuck Brook, a trained architect who for decades had been a leading development consultant, and Patrick Condon, a professor at the University of British Columbia's School of Architecture and Landscape Architecture and an influential critic and commentator.

Their argument—and given their backgrounds and influence, it was difficult to ignore—was that Southeast False Creek "should become a unique neighbourhood, not a copy of the [dense downtown] West End, Concord Pacific Place or anywhere else in Vancouver." Specifically, they urged that the new community should be low- to mid-rise, to differentiate it from the downtown highrises, to better integrate into the surrounding neighbourhood, and to maintain the sense that the inlet is the centre of a "basin," at the bottom of a slope coming down from the heights of Broadway, the principal east-west thoroughfare and the busiest and densest commercial strip outside of downtown Vancouver proper.

Brook says this wasn't a criticism of the downtown form. "We weren't arguing for something better; we were looking for something different." It was partly an urge to offer Vancouverites some choice, in housing and in the nature of the neighbourhood where they might choose to live. On the latter point, urban planners like to talk about granularity, referring to the degree to which streets and neighbourhoods are broken up into manageable, human-scale chunks. The planning guidelines across the creek in the downtown Vancouver peninsula had inadvertently destroyed the granularity in newly developed neighbourhoods. The City of Vancouver had decreed that if you wanted to build a tower—really, anything over 70 feet tall—you first had to assemble 125 feet of street frontage. The goal, in a tower-and-podium world, was to ensure that you had enough space to provide adequate separation between towers—again, to minimize shading on the ground and maximize view corridors. In Vancouver, developers tend to make all their money by selling view suites on the top floors of tall buildings, so there was a real incentive to assemble these big parcels and that meant the creation of a lot of long-block podium developments, without alleys and tiny side streets—the "fine-grain" detail that can help a community become more livable. Those lost features, Brook says, were among the urban elements the critics were hoping to recapture in the Olympic Village.

The third community of competence was the community itself. While Vancouver's planners had been planning and its designers designing, a large group of citizens and activists had become quite good at interacting with the City's planning processes. There were a great many people lined up to define and demand the elements of a vibrant, ecologically sound, and socially cohesive community. The Southeast False Creek Stewardship Group, for example, had been meeting non-stop since 1997.

In sum, you had a potentially beautiful piece of waterfront property in a city already renowned for its beauty and its development standards. And you had architects, planners, and activists all fired up to make sure that, whatever happened here, it was going to be good. But, of course, nobody was promising it would be easy.

Ken Bayne, then director of financial management and treasury at the City of Vancouver, says the other now-obvious aspect was that it would no longer be possible to break up the development and piece it out to a group of developers. Having lost two years in the planning, and with less than four years left until the whole new community needed to be in place for the Olympics, the only hope for making the deadline was if the entire site was developed by a single, and singularly resourceful, entity.

COME 2005, VANCOUVER'S deputy city manager and Olympic project manager Jody Andrews, who had made that first phone call inviting Millennium to bid, was well-regarded across the organization. Management loved him because, in the words of then-city manager Judy Rogers, Andrews was "one of the finest young people," the kind of guy you could count on to get a tough project finished in good order. Unionized workers loved him because, before coming back as deputy city manager, Andrews had quit his job as assistant city engineer in solidarity with his staff when the City had withdrawn the cherished four-day workweek. Shahram says that he, too, liked Andrews immediately. Dealing with Andrews, Shahram says he was reminded of Eric West, the City of Vancouver project manager who had worked so hard to help the Maleks succeed in their first City project on Cordova Street so many years before.

Even so, Shahram says, when Andrews made the Olympic pitch: "We weren't interested." The task was going to be impractically complex and impossibly rushed. Andrews had to make a few more calls before Shahram and Peter started taking the prospect seriously.

When they did, they called the architect Paul Merrick, whom they admired and who directed them into the capable hands of Roger Bayley. Bayley, a structural engineer, had co-founded Merrick Architecture with Paul in 1976, and had proved himself many times over as someone who could connect the ambition of soaring architecture to the practicalities of planning and construction. Bayley says now that Millennium had good reason to be skeptical about spending time working up an early proposal. First, while demonstrably up to the task, Millennium had kept a lower profile in a world then dominated by Concord Pacific, Concert Properties, and Wall Financial Corporation. Concord Pacific and the Wall group also had been more public in their efforts to craft a reputation as builders of energy-efficient and sustainable buildings.

More practically, Bayley says, the City was demanding a product mix that was going to make it impossible to make money. Bad enough that it was ruling against the simple and lucrative tall-tower form, but the City had also set out a requirement for one-third social housing, one-third moderate-priced housing, and one-third market housing. Every real estate economist in town agreed that, with that mix, there wouldn't be enough value for developers to cover their costs. Only when the City agreed to shift the mix to 80 percent market housing/20 percent social housing did Bayley and the brothers get busy preparing the first package for the Expression of Interest.

They made the first cut. Millennium was one of five developers invited to submit a full proposal, along with Concord Pacific, Concert, Wall, and Toronto-based Windmill Developments. Only Concord Pacific, Wall, and Millennium wound up staying in for the final competition.

The next stage was stressful, in part because the City had ranked the first-round Expressions of Interest and Millennium was sitting in third place, behind both Concord Pacific and Wall. As the brothers worked on the foundational calculations and general descriptions of the project, Bayley was working on his own numbers, and when he finished, he proposed that Millennium should offer the City $156 million for the land. In Bayley's recollection, "Shahram said, 'We really want this project.'" Millennium had lost out on some good opportunities in the past and the Maleks felt they had missed the boat in acquiring other properties at Southeast False Creek, as well as the Woodward's redevelopment. Perhaps, they said, this was one of those times when they needed to be bolder. As well, the Maleks say they were confident in their own estimates, which demonstrated that a well-executed project could support a higher residual land price. When they challenged Bayley to reconsider, he came back with a figure that was $20 million higher than his first estimate—closer to the Maleks' own calculations, but perhaps still not enough.

So, they asked him to crunch the numbers one more time. The Millennium bid finally went in at $193 million, $20 million more than

Concord Pacific's and $40 million more than Wall's—at that time, the highest price that anyone had paid for a patch of Vancouver's already inflated real estate. The Maleks admit to having had second thoughts even at the time.

On the morning it was to deliver the bid package, Millennium decided not to submit. It was offering an unprecedented amount for the land and the privilege of designing and building a complete and conspicuous community in less than three years. Both brothers are resolute in saying that it wasn't merely some Olympic dream. Peter says, "We knew that we could do a better job" than the other bidders. Still, it seemed too much, too fast, and too complicated. Let caution prevail.

And caution did prevail until about thirty minutes before the bid deadline. Helena Maurice, who had been Millennium's leading adminstrative support person for almost twenty years, picks up the story. At the eleventh hour, she says, the Maleks decided to submit the bid after all, triggering a frantic, last-minute rush. "We were collating packages right to the very end." Indeed, Maurice was still sorting pages in the back of the car on the way to City Hall, "and Shahram was driving as fast as he could—*legally*. I don't think he knew that I have motion sickness," Maurice says. When they pulled up in front of City Hall, she says, "Shahram grabbed everything and he ran—he's a jogger, anyway—and I was physically ill on the concrete of City Hall."

Shahram thought they might have missed the submission deadline by a couple of minutes, "but the City didn't disqualify us!" There seemed a tug of destiny and a compelling sense of purpose. "We knew we could do the job and build the best project," says Shahram. Given the breadth of work the brothers had done in Vancouver and beyond, even aside from Amir's history and expertise, Millennium could point to decades of relevant experience and proven competence.

Whatever the ultimate tipping point, Millennium's bid carried the day. Bayley says he thinks the deciding factor was the $20-million buffer that Shahram had insisted upon adding to the bid. "The price made it impossible for the City *not* to choose Millennium." But the Maleks say, with conviction, that it was their design of the community and the Olympic residences that got them on the shortlist in the first place. Theirs was always the value proposition, on every level.

The next hurdle—the inevitable, perennial hurdle—was financing. Raising money for a large development is seldom easy, even in a market as hot as Vancouver's was in the mid-2000s. Millennium had an unblemished track record with lenders but was looking for a *lot* of money—$750 million—for an incredibly complicated project that had to be completed in a ludicrously short time. The workplan included designing and building 1.2 million square feet of residential and commercial space—an eventual home to more than 4,900 people—and doing so in less than three years to deliver a village for more than 3,000 athletes for the 2010 Winter Olympics. In Vancouver, today, Peter says, "it takes more time than that just to get a permit for a single building." And because of the height restrictions and the City's insistence that this should be a dense, granular, European-style neighbourhood, Millennium was going to have to build eight city blocks, including condominiums, rental and social housing units, 70,000 square feet of commercial space, and a 45,000-square-foot community centre.

No worries. Development is fundamentally a business in which you accomplish the impractical at a breakneck pace. Besides, with the warm memories of Eric West in their minds and the reasonable voice of Jody Andrews in their ears, the Maleks say they were confident of the support they would receive from the City.

There was just one hiccup: the City had structured the deal in such a way that it was planning to retain actual ownership of the land until after the Olympics. Having made a solemn promise to the International Olympic Committee that it would provide the athletes' village on time and in good condition, City staffers worried about what would happen if the project started falling behind schedule. Then-director of financial management Ken Bayne says, "We needed to be able to step in at any time." So, the deal specified that they would lease the land to Millennium during the course of construction but hold title until after the Games. On that basis, the City said, Millennium could complete the development, turn the athletes' village over to the Olympic Committee for the course of the big event, and then take it back when the Games were over—at which point the City would transfer ownership of the land and Millennium could start delivering new condos, freehold, into the hands of happy buyers.

If the deal gave the City confidence, it did no such thing for the lending institutions where the Maleks had spent decades building up excellent credit. Banks like security. They particularly like a borrower to have enough equity that if they default on the loan, the banks can seize the underlying land together with enough assets to cover any outstanding loan amounts. Developers generally satisfy that condition by committing the land as collateral, and the banks wouldn't accept a three-year lease as nearly sufficient.

This condition was also not a surprise. It was one of the factors that had made the Maleks nervous about submitting a bid in the first place. Before starting the search for funding, they had approached some of the best real estate lawyers in their Rolodex, including Rob Brown, a respected lawyer and friend—all of whom shook their heads and told them the project was not financeable. They told the Maleks that no bank was going to part with three-quarters of a billion dollars when the only security was a short-term lease on some badly maintained industrial land. The Maleks' long-time real estate lawyer and consigliere, John Third, advised that Millennium would have to accept the terms as written in the proposal call, and rely on the City's goodwill and its assurance that the project was financeable based on its prior discussions with banks.

The Maleks sought to renegotiate the condition, but the City wouldn't bend. Officials said they had spoken to several Canadian banks and found they were all comfortable with the proposed structure. Which sounds credible. When the City of Vancouver was asking the question, the bankers were responding to a vast public body that did, in fact, own the land. But when the Maleks asked, they got the answer their lawyers had said to expect. They went to all the banks that they had worked with for years and each time they received the same dour shake of the head. They also appealed to the City to change the structure—receiving the self-same dour refusal.

Sam Sullivan, who was mayor during this period, says he was sympathetic at the time, but "there were no options in my mind, because of the timing." The City was facing enormous pressure: "We had three years to turn a dirt site into a city. It's hard to imagine." They also had set up the original call for Expression of Interest based on this short-lease format, so, while "there was a temptation to change everything again, once the Request for Proposals was done, if we'd changed it, we would have had to run the whole process over again." Still, Sullivan was concerned that, "this was going to be the only major Canadian development without Canadian financing. In retrospect, I wish I had pushed harder [to remove the short-term leasing requirement]. It ended up being a nightmare."

There was a moment of excitement—and perhaps a sign that the City's for-lease financing scheme might be acceptable after all—when Millennium applied to the Caisse de dépôt et placement du Québec, the biggest institutional investor in that province. Millennium had an excellent track record with the Caisse, having completed three large residential towers in Burnaby with Caisse funding. Their lending team said yes.

Yes!

But given the size of the loan, the file needed final approval from the Caisse's board of directors, and as the story was reported back to the Maleks, some of the board members had painful memories of an earlier Olympian promise. The 1976 Summer Olympics in Montreal had been sold as a can't-lose prospect. The mayor of the day, Jean Drapeau, said famously that "the Montreal Olympics can no more have a deficit than a man can have a baby." Which is why it's so easy to find caricatures of a pregnant Jean Drapeau. The 1976 Olympics ran wildly over budget, leaving a debt of $1.5 billion, a little over $8 billion in 2023 dollars The last payment on that debt was posted in December 2006, three decades after the event and mere months before the Maleks were getting their loan applications rejected everywhere. So, having first said yes, the Caisse slammed the door. In the end, Even the Canadian Mortgage and Housing Corporation declined to insure the financing on the basis that it, too, already had too much Olympic exposure.

Millennium's next stop was New York. A well-respected Vancouver-based commercial realtor had introduced Millennium to Fortress Investments Group LLC, which bills itself as "a leading, highly diversified global investment manager," but which is more often described as "a hedge fund," or, if the describer is in a bad mood, "a predatory lender." In 2007, Fortress was flush with cash and had just bought Intrawest, the owner-operator of Whistler Blackcomb and a lush portfolio of destination-ski resorts in Canada and the United States. Fortress apparently thought that doubling down on a project related to the Whistler Olympics was a good idea, especially because the lender charged Millennium a staggering variable interest rate of prime plus 6 percent, which wound up averaging 10.5 percent—two or three times what the banks were charging at the time. Peter says, "It was not ideal, but there were no other options." It was one of the many times they might have harkened back to Amir's example of having assumed difficult projects on which other contractors had submitted lower bids but failed, and then had figured out a way to make them work—not just to complete them, but to make money.

The high interest rate wasn't the only problem. Fortress also demanded further security. So, after significant additional pleading with the City, in which the Maleks pointed out that it was the leasing format that created the problem, the City agreed to co-sign for $193 million, to make up for the fact that the Olympic Village land could not be used as security. The promise didn't offset any of Millennium's additional lending costs, but it got the project moving.

Amid the stress of dealing with the hard-bargaining financiers from Fortress, the brothers were much happier to renew their acquaintance with another New Yorker, Robert Stern, with whom Millennium had enjoyed such success on their elegant and triumphant West Vancouver projects. The Dean Emeritus of the Yale School of Architecture and the grandfather of post-modernism, Stern has his critics—no good architect could expect not to—but his portfolio is full of stately and beautiful work. The Maleks considered him a perfect candidate to design the most prominent building along the Southeast False Creek waterfront, so in September 2006, they invited him to Vancouver to contemplate the site and its possibilities. Given their excellent experiences with him in West Vancouver, they were delighted to send him out on a walking tour with *Vancouver Sun* reporter John Mackie, a former rock 'n' roll critic who, thanks to a sharp eye and a deep and obvious affection for the city, had transformed himself into an

Peter and Shahram early days, Tehran.

Peter and mother Mahin getting ready to leave for
Holmewood House after putting on school uniform,
London, UK, 1960s.

Shahram, during school holidays, Brighton, UK, 1960s.

Holmewood House Preparatory School, Langton Green, Kent, UK.

Peter Malek, Holmewood House School photo, 1960s.

Shahram, Amir, Marjan, and Peter in Rome during school holidays, 1960s.

Shahram Malek, Holmewood House
School photo, 1960s.

Velodrome, Sports Hall, Swimming Pool, at Aryamehr Sports Complex, Tehran 1974.

The 105,000-seat Stadium, designed by Skidmore, Owings and Merril of Chicago, and Abdol-Aziz Farmanfarmaian architects, part of the Olympic-standard Aryamehr Sports Complex, Tehran 1974.

(Left to right) Peter, Mahin, Amir, Maryam, Shahram, and Marjan at uncle's wedding in Sussex, UK, 1978.

(Left to right) Mother Mahin and sister Ellie at the family's Caspian Sea summer retreat, a thickly forested 25-acre waterfront estate with a winding driveway leading to the hilltop villa, 1978.

Shahram at his desk in the Parc des Princes project office, Tehran, 1979. He was the last member of the family remaining in Iran, and left the country after the Parc des Princes apartments were handed over to purchasers in August 1980, almost 2 years after the Revolution.

Vanak Park complex in Tehran, designed by iconic Iranian architect Abdol-Aziz Farmanfarmaian, 1979.

Parc des Princes complex in Tehran, designed by architects Giuseppe Barsanti & Vico Magistretti of Milan, considered one of the most influential mid-century architects, 1979.

Peter (left) and Shahram (right) in front of Shahram's Folkestone Way apartment, West Vancouver, BC, 1982.

Peter, Amir (seated), and Shahram in Amir's office at family's Paris home, 1980s.

Left to right: Peter, Amir, Maryam, Shahram, and Mahin (seated), at Amir and Mahin's Paris home, 1980s. The home was bought by Amir for Mahin before the Iranian Revolution, which turned out to be fortuitous since it was the only family asset outside of Iran after the Revolution.

Armeco renovation of the Terminal Building of Victoria International Airport, which tripled the size of its facilities, Victoria, BC, 1985.

Langley Memorial Hospital expansion project, Langley, BC, late 1980s.

Formal gardens and grand staircase at Millennium's City-in-the-Park master-planned seven-tower community, Award for Excellence in Urban Development, Burnaby, BC, 1997.

Barry Rice, Peter Malek, Robert A.M. Stern, and Shahram Malek, outside Millennium's refurbished Province Building, 1998.

Robert A.M. Stern and Lawrence Doyle–designed Edgewater residential tower, West Vancouver, BC, 2000.

Left to right: Bob Rennie, Peter Malek, Amir Malek, and Shahram Malek, at the Lumiere tower roof topping event, 2001.

Lumiere residential tower and townhomes, Vancouver West End, BC, 2002.

Millennium's restored Province Building, a seven-storey Edwardian Classical Revival commercial building, Vancouver, BC.

Millennium office entrance in the renovated Province Building, 2002.

Shahram and Peter Malek with Burnaby Mayor Derek Corrigan at groundbreaking of City-in-the-Park Tower 7, Belvedere, Burnaby, BC, 2004.

One Madison Avenue, three concrete residential high-rises of up to 30 storeys in Burnaby, BC, winner of Grand Georgie Award, 2005.

Shahram and Peter Malek with Simon Fraser University President Dr. Michael Stevenson and UniverCity President Michael Geller at the groundbreaking for One University Crescent on Burnaby Mountain, BC, 2005.

One University Crescent on Burnaby Mountain, winner of Grand Georgie Award for Best Multi-Family Development.

Shahram Malek, Robert A.M. Stern, and Peter Malek in front of Water's Edge
Development, West Vancouver, BC, August, 2006.

Water's Edge Development, West Vancouver, BC, National SAM Award for Best
Multi-Family Housing in Canada.

L' Hermitage mixed-use development, Vancouver, BC, comprised of a luxury hotel, residences, social housing, and shops. 2010 Housing Award, CMHC, Recognizing Leadership from the Private Sector.

Shahram Malek, lawyer John Third (seated), and Peter Malek preparing for handover of the Olympic Village to VANOC ahead of schedule; Millennium's Olympic Village office, September 2009.

Lawyer Mitch Gropper acting for the City of Vancouver (left) and Peter Malek (right) preparing to sign over Millennium properties and personal assets (row of yellow folders) to the City. Farris LLP Boardroom, April 2011.

Olympic Village Square, Vancouver, BC.

Arthur Erickson and Nick Milkovich–designed "Canada House" in Vancouver's celebrated Olympic Village, 2010.

Aerial photo of Millennium's Olympic Village in the foreground to the right of Science World building. The Olympic Village was the catalyst for subsequent developments in South East False Creek.

Shahram, Amir, and Peter Malek at the dedication of a plaque honouring Millennium's development of the Olympic Village, December 11, 2014.

Merchants Bank building, 1920s, which Millennium has renovated and now houses Millennium's Vancouver headquarters.

A touch of Paris in Vancouver. The imposing "Beaux Arts" structure was constructed in 1913 by renowned architects Somervell and Putnam, and originally housed the Montreal-based Merchants Bank. The building was constructed in the "Temple Bank" style, reminiscent of classical Parisian buildings, symbolizing strength, solidity, and prosperity. Extensive preservation, upgrading work was completed by Millennium in 2020.

The 47-storey Triomphe tower in Burnaby, BC, 340 luxurious homes, designed by CDA Architects, completed 2020.

The first two towers in the 3-tower, up-to-47-storey Etoile development in Burnaby, BC, 2023.

architectural and cultural commentator. Mackie's report of that stroll was marvelous, with the typically critical Stern casting aspersions on some of Vancouver's favourite buildings. But the story also lit a fire under the local architectural community.

Stern's most memorable criticism was this: "I think there are too many glass towers in Vancouver. That's one reason they all look alike, there's nothing to write on, so to speak. So, you get funny little hats on these buildings, and sometimes you get strange balconies. There are more triangular balconies in Vancouver than any place else I've ever been. I wonder if they're storing arrowheads on these balconies."

He went on: "They [the ubiquitous glass towers] try to look different, but somehow they all look exactly alike. So, I think there's a kind of boring uniformity. None of them are really bad, they're not ugly, but [there are] too many identical things."

Stern further complained about the not-very-granular line of tower-and-podium developments running through and away from the Marathon properties on Coal Harbour: "When you go out to Stanley Park you have one after another after another [of these] giant high rises, but [West Georgia] street is so pedestrian unfriendly and uninviting. It could have been done—should have been done—in a very different way."

There is truth in those criticisms. Stern wasn't the first person to complain about the overabundance of green glass in Vancouver's skyline, and no one who has ever walked that section of West Georgia would call it a pedestrian paradise. But the New Yorker's harsh judgment drew fierce and defensive criticism. There was lots of indignation, lots of sneering criticism of another community that Stern had designed—the Disneyfied village in Celebration, Florida, which an earlier *Sun* architectural writer, Robin Ward, had derided as "a fake-heritage small town, straight out of a Norman Rockwell

illustration, that's designed to appeal to nostalgic baby boomers."
But Stern had not come to Vancouver to make apologies, for his criticisms or for the sold-out development in Celebration, which, he
noted, excited buyers had "embraced ... with open arms." And he
added, "I think the same principles we used there are what are being
used in the Olympic Village site: small blocks, keeping the parking
away." Again, this was true: those *were* the principles that had already
been developed for planning Olympic Village. But the accuracy of
Stern's comments didn't make them any easier to hear. And no one
asked for further detail about the modern timeless buildings he had
described for the brothers; they just fretted that someone might turn
Vancouver's planned showpiece of urban environmentalism into a
Disney World suburb, which was far from the truth.

Things got worse when the *Sun* quoted marketing guru Bob Rennie
interpreting Stern's intentions, saying, "The whole idea is, instead of
defaulting to this ultra-contemporary [look], to build a classic fishing
village." Looking at the range and locational sensitivity of Stern's previous work, and knowing the contemporary images that he had been
describing to the Maleks, this was a characterization that begged to be
misinterpreted further. And sure enough, when resistant members of
the City of Vancouver's Urban Design Panel started complaining about
their preconceptions of a New Yorker's designs for a neo-classical fishing village, Stern graciously excused himself from the commission.

Soon after, Shahram sat down for coffee with the City's senior
urban designer, Scot Hein, in a meeting room in L'Hermitage.
Shahram was greatly disappointed to have lost the services of an architect he admires, even if Stern was only ever going to design one of
the buildings in the village. So, even without a specific plan to try to
reverse the Stern decision, Shahram had brought along a Robert Stern
coffee-table book. He started sharing favourite images, giving Hein

the opening to ask what Shahram liked best about Stern's work—and Shahram pointed to the details and the materiality. Having spent so much of his childhood in the UK and Europe, Shahram loved the classic sense of proportionality, which he envisioned being conveyed in this new project in a modern style. Hein said, "Great, we just have to make sure the rules allow for that aspiration."

Hein says now that there followed a quick and collaborative process to reassure the planning gurus, Vancouver's plentiful architectural hobbyists and critics, and the press. The frequent Millennium collaborator Stu Lyon from GBL Architects recast the planning scheme into ten principles—guidelines rather than constraints—that stressed accessibility and light, even to the extent of having skylights that transmit daylight to underground spaces. Hein, whose own writing either influenced or has been influenced by the principles in question, says: "It was a seminal moment in Vancouver architectural history."

Still, the design debate raged on. Shahram says, "Some in the City wanted the buildings to *appear* sustainable. They even suggested the corrugated Granville Island buildings as a preferred example." But one of Millennium's leading architects, Paul Merrick, argued passionately that the underlying precepts of sustainability have been around as long as history and that many buildings around the world and across the ages dealt well with issues of climate and livability without having to *look* sustainable.

The brothers countered utilitarian or industrial images with examples of curving glass and continuing balconies, such as those on the Mediterranean Marina Baie des Anges in Nice, France, or the luxurious Yve Apartments project in Melbourne, Australia. They also suggested—and ultimately delivered—arcades for the buildings fronting the plaza, to provide the classic feel and vibrant street life so common in pedestrian-friendly European capitals.

Thanks, perhaps, to the misunderstanding about Robert Stern's role and vision, there also was much talk about choosing modern versus classical architecture, and about West Coast versus other forms. Shahram goes on, "With the City's other aspirations for a low-profile, self-supporting neighbourhood, we challenged our architectural team to design something functional, alluring, and timeless, and they rose to the task beautifully."

With the clock ticking, there followed a flurry of planning and design—and then an explosion of construction energy. There are comparable planned communities in BC, some even bigger than this project. You might look at Dockside Green in Victoria or UniverCity on Burnaby Mountain as planned, self-contained communities that achieved remarkably high standards for environmental sustainability. Like Olympic Village, UniverCity was designed to be complete and integrated, with all the services and amenities necessary to serve the local community. For sheer size and architectural ambition, you could look at the Marathon Lands along Coal Harbour. And, of course, the Concord Pacific developments in Yaletown and on the old Expo lands are more than twice as big as the Olympic Village site. But all of those communities were built over a long period, one building at a time—each being pre-sold and eased into a proven market. The community centres, child-care centres, parks, and other amenities were also added as financing allowed—or after the population had arrived and the demand grew insatiable. Only Olympic Village was conceived, designed, built, and delivered—in a single, fully functional burst—in thirty months.

Hein says that such a thing—1.5 million square feet of commercial and residential space, housing, and shops for 4,900 people and amenities including a 45,000-square-foot community centre and the completion of Vancouver's almost 30-kilometre seawall—simply couldn't be done today. "It was fifteen years of city building in three. It's an absolute miracle they pulled it off."

The project also happened during what Hein describes as "a beautiful moment" at the City, a time when teams and expertise had been forged over many years and through many projects, including the post-Expo boom. There was also an uncommon degree of trust. First, Hein says Millennium, while driving relentlessly to an impossible deadline, was also accommodating, giving architects room to do their best work.

And there was much work to do. In the early days, Hein says, there were three hundred architects all drawing concurrently. The workload all but overwhelmed some of Vancouver's largest firms and most-experienced practitioners. The core team came from Merrick Architecture, with Paul Merrick, Greg Borowski, Mitch Sakumoto, and Rob Ciccozzi, and GBL Architects, led by the Maleks' long-time collaborator Stu Lyon.

On the waterfront, the team faced two challenges: the prime residential site for which the Maleks had originally intended to commission Robert Stern; and the community centre site. Millennium recruited Arthur Erickson and Nick Milkovich for both, facing down complaints from the Vancouver Parks Board, which didn't have the world-renowned Erickson on their internal list of recommended architects. The Maleks also encouraged a collaboration with Walter Francl, who *was* on the Parks Board list, again fending off a municipal authority government that kept pointing out that it was in a hurry to meet an Olympic deadline but, nevertheless, kept setting out roadblocks.

There followed what Hein characterizes as a prolonged period of "crazy just-in-time work," with the City accepting partially completed proposals for rezoning and the Urban Design Panel signing off on drawings that were still very much in progress. Hein says that he met with Millennium's talented landscape architect Peter Kreuk of Durante Kreuk almost daily for eighteen months. Working with the whole extended Millennium team—what Hein calls "mirroring"—"we just had to stay collegial and work closely together."

Rob Ciccozzi was quoted on this point in *The Challenge Series,* a seven-book set that Roger Bayley organized to memorialize the project. Ciccozzi said: "We went through four or five iterations on Parcel 6 [the large block on the northwest side of the development] with the client [the Maleks] sitting right next to us. We'd do eight-hour stints—they'd bring in lunch. I've got the tracing paper; we're coming up with solutions then and there. I've never had to do that before. I enjoyed it to some degree, but it was draining. It was a lot of pressure." The Maleks were very hands-on.

Crediting city manager Judy Rogers and deputy city manager Jody Andrews, Hein says, "we were also left alone by the City's senior managers. The bureaucracy knew we had to be nimble, and it came down to having confidence in those in the trenches. That's the only way we were able to pull it off. Everyone stepped up and people were given permission to do their best work. It was exhilarating—so positive. And we made a neighbourhood that all Vancouver could be proud of."

As Millennium and the designers were working on the vision of what would be built, others were preparing the ground—no small feat on its own. The site was a contaminated mess, requiring the largest soil remediation in Vancouver history, which added more than $25 million to the cost of the project and also added to the delays. This, too, is a sore point for Millennium, another point on which it had hoped to negotiate relief, even if it had not been promised in the original agreement.

The provincial government had paid to clean up industrial contamination of the Expo lands, and the City hoped the Province would absorb that liability once again. But both the Province and the City ducked responsibility on the southeast shore, leaving Millennium to manage—and pay for—the work. And there was a lot of work. It's always difficult to convey the actual size of this kind of endeavour. If you say 160,000 cubic metres, it doesn't really compute for the average reader. So, people are inclined to divide that number by something more manageable: a favourite is the Olympic-sized swimming pool. But really, who knows how big a pile of poisoned soil you need to fill an Olympic-sized pool, much less sixty-four of them. So, we're left with the image, the noise, and (here's something people understand) the traffic congestion of 140 dump trucks a day driving in, lining up, and loading up. Every one of those trucks then had to line up again at the industrial-sized "wheel wash" facility that sprayed contaminants off the trucks' tires and undercarriages. And then drivers set off in all directions: to the Vancouver landfill in Burns Bog; to the Tsawwassen landfill; or, for the material that was really bad, to the provincial hazardous waste facility in Princeton, BC—a 280-kilometre drive, a good three hours in each direction.

Actual construction didn't so much begin as break out. Millennium engaged two general contractors, Metro-Can and ITC, whose work was overseen by Millennium's own general manager of development and construction, Hank Jasper. In no time, there were 1,500 people on the site and thirteen tower cranes. The crane operators all got special training on how to work safely in this congested crane forest, and they had to get used to communicating on six different radio channels, while learning to manage an anti-collision system that had never been used in Canada.

Jasper, who had "six or seven" project managers reporting to him, says this kind of project would usually take ten years, at least. "We had under three years: then they were going to turn on all the lights and expect everything would all operate together." His project motto became, "There is no Plan B!"

"There could be no backing away from anything," he says. Jasper became known—or perhaps he was already known—for being tough and temperamental, and having what Roger Bayley describes as "a particular management style—it was management by two-by-four." If someone was not measuring up to Jasper's expectations, Bayley says, "Hank would take people into the boards and skate away, smiling."

Told of this comment, Jasper laughs and says, "I like to think of myself as a softie." But he remembers Bayley saying one day, "You can't be going nuclear all the time." Still chuckling, Jasper says, "Hopefully, I picked my spots."

There were lots of spots to pick. It was a busy time in the construction industry, not just in False Creek but all over the city, and Millennium was having to compete for subcontractors. Jasper says one of the subs' favourite pastimes is to identify "extras"—anything that they can argue wasn't part of the original bid price. Everyone in town knew they had extra leverage on this project because, as Jasper said, there really *was* no Plan B. The deadline was immovable, so Millennium's bargaining strategies couldn't include trying to wait anyone out. In a hot market, labour was scarce and increasingly expensive, and commodity and component prices were also rising at the rate of 1 or 2 percent a month, a significant acceleration of the inflation that was already affecting construction when the brothers were making their original estimates.

The Maleks, and no small group of additional critics, also point to the City's ambition to create a model sustainable community as having had a strongly inflationary impact on the whole project. Millennium certainly incorporated an unprecedented number of environmental and energy-saving innovations, the majority of which were encouraged or outright imposed by the City *after* design and construction got underway. For example, the whole development is served by a Neighbourhood Energy Utility that relies on waste heat from nearby City sewage lines, supplemented at times of high demand by natural gas. It was the first application of this technology in a dense urban environment anywhere in North America.

Among the other innovative or experimental sustainability add-ons, there are heat exchangers in individual buildings that harvest waste heat from cooling systems, from cars in the parkade, from appliances, and, in some buildings, from solar panels, and use that energy to pre-heat hot water. There are green roofs, including roof-top gardens and rainwater collection systems that provide the water for toilet flushing and outdoor watering. (Almost all other homes in the city use potable water that has been treated, expensively, to be safe to drink, but is then just flushed down the toilet or sprayed on the lawn—the two biggest uses of water in the broader system.) There is highly efficient radiant heating and cooling and energy-efficient lighting throughout. And every building in the development was designed with an eye to modern "passive" standards—which is to say, they are designed to create a bright, comfortable, indoor environment by taking best advantage of the energy of the sun. In a world where energy has been extremely cheap, we have become tolerant of buildings that are cheap to construct but expensive to operate. Glass, for example, is both a terrible insulator when you're trying to keep heat in and an uncomfortable magnifier when you're trying to keep heat out. Passive design standards call for smaller windows on the south side of buildings, where direct sunlight causes rooms to overheat, and larger ones on the north, where you want the light. Olympic Village buildings also have daylight in corridors and staircases. These encourage people to use the stairs, rather than the elevator, even as they put more "eyes on the street," because people who are bathed in natural light while walking up and down staircases also have a bird's eye view of what's happening outside.

Roger Bayley heaps praise upon the project's sustainability advisor, the late Andy Kesteloo, for the success of the project's broad, integrated, and unprecedented array of sustainable elements. Millennium hired Kesteloo to oversee and champion the green-building components, and Bayley says that Kesteloo, a long-standing board member on the Canada Green Building Council, "was one of the few people in the sustainable building industry ... who could connect the cost implications of green components with a really good understanding of long-term value."

For Kesteloo as much as for the sharp-eyed and sharp-pencilled Peter Malek, you had to make an economic case for every innovation, no matter how apparently green it seemed on the surface. Kesteloo died suddenly of a brain aneurism in 2007, not much more than a year into the project. But the City continued to pile on demands and, Bayley says, even without Kesteloo's ongoing guidance, Millennium continued to incorporate the new ideas.

Hein and Bayley have an unusually rosy recollection of all this innovation. Hein acknowledges that the City never stopped dreaming up environmental innovations that would further complicate the project. He also says, "Millennium was *so* accommodating." Bayley, too, says the green features added complexity to an already overwhelming endeavour, but (alone among those on the Millennium team) he rejects the notion that the sustainability features drove up costs—and he credits Hein for being a good collaborator.

For example, when the City began to press for efficient but potentially expensive exterior-insulated wall assemblies, Bayley agreed, but only if the City also adjusted the allowable building envelope so

THE OLYMPIC CHALLENGE   143

Millennium wouldn't be stuck with an extra cost. Normally, developers will tuck insulation between the studs on exterior walls: you wind up with something that is not as energy efficient, but you save space. At Olympic Village, the City agreed to increase the allowable building envelope by the width of that extra insulation, so, Bayley says, Millennium got to deliver a better, more energy-efficient product while not inflating the cost.

Bayley and Hein also maintain a romantic view of the plentiful sustainability features, saying that whenever they could demonstrate that something could be added at no cost, Peter was consistently supportive. Bayley goes so far as to say that "no other developer would have allowed it," and that Millennium's competitors "would have 'value engineered' those features right out of there." But, Bayley says, the Maleks never stopped trying to improve the project.

The Maleks are happy enough to acknowledge their good management of the many innovations that the City imposed upon the project, but Peter says flatly that it's "nonsense" that these demands didn't add expense. Cost containment is a critical function in all development and Peter is renowned as someone who keeps his pencil razor-sharp. As Bayley says, "there was never a drawing that Peter hadn't spent three or four hours on, scribbling notes"—not just monitoring expense but commenting on every detail, down to which way the shower doors would swing. Peter remembers the hard work; it's always been part of his practice, although this project was considerably more intense. But Bayley's enthusiasm notwithstanding, Peter is categorical that the City's insistence upon environmental innovation, in the midst of a project that was already unfolding at breakneck pace, slowed the project and inflated the costs. Millennium's development manager Jasper ultimately estimated the cost increase to be $39 million.

There were occasions when even Bayley resisted upgrades. One example arose when the Maleks said they wanted to add limestone cladding on the concrete columns at the base of the buildings along the northern, creek-facing side of the project. Bayley says that his long-time partner, Paul Merrick, who also was instrumental in providing design guidelines, is a big fan of raw concrete, which, done well, can make for a very attractive exterior. But the Maleks were undeterred. Walking down the waterfront street in the completed village, they point to the resilience and longevity of limestone, which is less likely to stain, and which can retain its richness and lustre for centuries. "We wanted to build something beautiful, and something that would last—that would stand up," Shahram says.

Bayley's other complaint arose from the waterfront building that came to be known as Canada House because it's where the Canadian Olympic team stayed during the Games. This prestige site was originally excluded from the Olympic package; although prominently located on the northwest corner of the Olympic Village property, it was a complicated site with a high water table and required special pilings to secure the foundation. Given that there would be sufficient space to house Olympic athletes even without this site, the City had agreed that the Maleks could complete this most valuable waterfront section later than the other buildings, perhaps even after the Olympics. This made sense from a logistical and marketing perspective: you generally want to build and sell the most valuable properties last because they benefit most from the increase in value that comes as a development of this magnitude is coming closer to conclusion.

After the other work was well underway, however, Jody Andrews called Shahram and requested a review. This being the premier location in the village, Andrews said it would mean a lot to the City if the Maleks could proceed so that this estimable spot could be used as the home for Canada's own athletes. True to its record for accommodation, Millennium agreed to add the construction of these two buildings with their extensive underground parking and other amenities into an already-frantic project schedule. The Maleks were increasingly confident in their own process, and they still thought they and the City were on the same team. Completing this high-profile additional project seemed like goodwill in the bank.

They considered it a bonus, at this point, to be able to add Arthur Erickson and his team into the mix—for inspiration and execution. Erickson was eighty years old and no longer spending every waking hour at the drawing table, but the Maleks convinced him to take over design of the prime waterfront building site originally planned for Robert Stern, and Erickson pronounced himself delighted at the prospect.

As the story is told now, when they were discussing possible designs for the building that would be Canada House, there was a deck of cards on the table and Arthur reached down and gave the deck a twist, so the "walls" of the once-tight rectangle now sloped dynamically on all four sides. Everyone loved the idea, and Erickson's long-time collaborator Nick Milkovich worked closely with Larry Doyle to give the inspiration an architectural expression on the page. But there were challenges in executing the design. Erickson's twist meant that each floor was slightly offset, so the buildings morph as they rise. This meant that Millennium couldn't use conventional cladding. Instead, the architects worked with the suppliers to develop a custom metal-and-glass panel, which they dubbed "fishscale" for its reflective texture. Bayley says the two buildings on this lot ultimately required 7,447 of these exquisite panels, each one unique. That made it incredibly difficult and expensive to craft the moveable sunshades that were required to meet a passive-design element that the City imposed on Arthur Erickson's challenging form. Peter fought hard to have the sunshades removed, but the City agreed only to a minor modification.

Bayley concludes: "We could have hung a BMW outside every window (as a sunshade) and saved money." Even worse, as Peter predicted, the sunshades were so difficult to use and expensive to keep up that the ultimate owners quickly stopped using them. It was money for nothing.

By the middle of 2007, with trucks dumping, cranes flying, and crews already working on the waterfront section that would ultimately connect 30 kilometres of Vancouver's unmatched urban seawall, the public was fully aware that something heroic and fabulous was happening at Olympic Village.

Come October, when Bob Rennie's marketing team threw open the doors on what he describes as "an Epcot-quality" pre-sale marketing centre, the lineup stretched around the block. Real estate agents had hired college students to hold a place to ensure they got first crack at the 302 units available in the first phase—one student reported sitting there for five days. With suites listed between $450,000 and $3.5 million, some people grumbled that the price point was a bit high. But Yvonne Dawson, Rennie's sales manager, says that most people just raved about the location, the views, the proximity to services, the standards of sustainability (and therefore long-term affordability), and the fact that every new owner was buying a little piece of Olympic glory. "It was so exciting," Dawson says. They quickly sold out the first building, and by Christmas, more than 250 buyers had put down their deposits, even though it would be almost three years before the condos were available.

THE MILLENNIUM PROJECT was running full bore by the time the financial world started to flutter, nervously, in the run-up to what would become the subprime mortgage crisis. The first unignorable warning came in June 2007, when the New York investment house Bear Stearns announced that two of its hedge funds had imploded, toppling over dominos that would lead to the institution's collapse the next year and trigger a world-wide financial meltdown.

Millennium construction manager Hank Jasper got an early warning of trouble in 2008 when Fortress began complaining about the Olympic project missing deadlines or busting budgets.

It's common enough for a project to miss some targets, and every lender has an incentive to track shortcomings that might threaten their investment. But by the time Fortress was compiling its list, it was in deep financial trouble. In that threatening financial environment, Fortress sent an unusually long list of complaints about missed deadlines and overruns that stunned Jasper and the Millennium team: "Thirty-five pages of defaults!" Jasper said, still irked by the memory of the hedge fund's missive. For someone managing a project of this complexity, under this much pressure, it was clearly an affront. And Jasper had good reason to complain. To Ken Bayne, the city's director of financial management, who was responsible for overseeing the financial side of the project, the Fortress list of complaints were "spurious."

You could see the problem. Fortress had agreed to lend Millennium up to $750 million, advanced as needed during the course of the project, and when they made the deal, it was still pretty easy for a hedge fund like Fortress to raise funds, in North America or Asia, at a reasonable rate in the low single digits and loan them again to Millennium at 10.5 percent. Easy money.

Suddenly, though, raising money got very hard. Under pressure on many of its ventures, Fortress's share price lost 92 percent of its value in 2008, leaving the principals distracted and the company within a hair of being delisted from the New York Stock Exchange. It's perfectly possible that Fortress wasn't withholding funds from Millennium because the work was going badly; they were withholding funds because they simply didn't have the money they had promised to lend, and their own credit worthiness had tanked so badly that no one would help cover those commitments.

No matter the actual cause, Fortress—which to this point had advanced $320 million—turned off the tap, leaving Millennium to go on a fresh search for funding on a project that had been nearly impossible to finance in the first place. So, the Maleks did the only thing they could. They went back to the City of Vancouver, explained the circumstances, and asked for support—beginning with $100 million in bridge financing that they could use to keep construction on schedule. The City gave its approval—quietly—with a unanimous vote in a closed Finance Committee meeting. At least, they tried to do it quietly. But the meeting fell exactly a month before the 2008 municipal election, and someone snapped up one of the briefing documents and passed it along to journalist Gary Mason, who promptly reported the whole deal in his column in the *Globe and Mail*. Suddenly, Millennium, which had managed to keep a low profile for decades, was the centrepiece in a political firestorm.

If you set aside the Maleks, the principals in this contretemps were the two leading candidates for mayor. The prevailing favourite was Peter Ladner, veteran councillor, scion of an old and powerful Vancouver family, and a long-time banner carrier for the centre-right municipal political party, the Non-Partisan Association (NPA). Ladner was something of a golden boy, founder of the popular *Business in Vancouver* news magazine, which added to his business bona fides. He was also an avid cyclist and outspoken environmentalist. So, despite his long-time NPA association, he had a surprising amount of support in the political middle, and he easily supplanted Sam Sullivan as the NPA's mayoral nominee. Inconveniently, however, Ladner was also chair of the Finance Committee that had approved the $100-million advance to Millennium.

Ladner's challenger was Gregor Robertson, a handsome young New Democratic Party Member of the British Columbia Legislative Assembly with a similar claim to both environmental consciousness and credibility in business. Robertson had made a fortune as the founder of the organic juice company Happy Planet before sweeping into provincial politics in 2005. His jump onto the municipal scene came as a bit of a surprise, and in the middle of October 2008, a month before the election, he was trailing in the polls. The biggest story in the campaign to that point cast Robertson as a transit scofflaw—first because he had ridden too far on the rapid transit SkyTrain without topping up his ticket, and second because, after he was caught, he hadn't paid the $175 ticket. It was hardly earth-shattering, but the story seemed to be doing real damage to Robertson's integrity score.

And even Robertson might have admitted that Ladner was a great candidate: experienced, smart, and surprisingly "green" for an establishment-party representative. (He is, today, the chair of the David Suzuki Foundation.) Ladner and Robertson were both getting media attention for showing up to campaign events on their bicycles. But the polls were clear: advantage Ladner.

The leak, and the ensuing brouhaha, "really changed the complexion of the entire election," says the *Globe's* Mason. Robertson and his Vision Vancouver running mates accused Ladner and his NPA "cronies" of being naive, incompetent, and sneaky—of ramming through a risky Olympic commitment, of managing the project badly, and then of doing a dubious financing deal in secret.

This was pure politics. People rise quickly to suspicion anytime any-thing happens in an in-camera meeting. In this case, the City rules are clear that major financial decisions have to be discussed and decided privately, especially when they involve contractual arrangements with partners outside the City. And with the exception of whoever slipped Mason the minutes, everyone from Ladner on down had followed the rules. As well, there was never any question the matter would have become public ultimately, but it was a happy conve-nience for Robertson and his Vision co-campaigners that they could make the bailout look questionable because it had occurred behind closed doors. It didn't matter that four Vision councillors were also in the room at the time and had supported the decision unanimously. And even though their participation was well reported at the time, Robertson and his running mates had little trouble pinning the whole thing on Ladner.

Vision Vancouver's accusations of secrecy and financial incompe-tence worked like a charm, resetting the campaign narrative. Everyone forgot Robertson's transit transgressions and spent the weeks leading up to the municipal vote asking Ladner why the City was pamper-ing big-money developers. Mason says, "Nobody knows one hundred percent what made people vote [in the following election]. But Vision Vancouver talked about [the Olympic Village financing] as a pivotal inflection point in the campaign," which Robertson won in a walk and which reduced the NPA to one seat. In reference to Ladner and his team, Mason concludes, "It certainly didn't help them."

No surprise. If you Google the term "Olympic boondoggle," you get 660,000 results in less than half a second—everything from newspa-per, magazine, and television stories to YouTube videos, podcasts, and academic studies. It's not just that corruption and influence-peddling stories are common in the Olympic sphere; it's the predictable cost overruns that seem to burden anyone bold enough to volunteer their city as a venue. (The happy Canadian exception of Calgary, site of the financially successful 1988 Winter Olympics, is still overshadowed by the crushing debt left behind from the Montreal Summer Games twelve years earlier.) In BC, many pundits had already been predicting that the Vancouver-Whistler party would be an economic catastrophe, so there was a ready appetite for a round of indignant "Olympic bailout" stories. Consider the tone of this short snippet in *Maclean's* magazine at the beginning of January 2009, just two months after the election:

> Quietly yet inevitably, the City of Vancouver has approached the province and feds to bail it out of the $1 billion Olympic Village funding scandal, in which developers of the village foolishly got on the hook for a $750-million loan from a Wall Street hedge fund. The loan has gone sour, the project is already $125 million over budget and debt servicing costs have hit $35 million per year. Meantime, the resale value of the units is crashing, meaning taxpayers would likely recover a fraction of the original value of the project. No wonder, then, that some are drawing comparisons to the 1976 funding debacle in Montreal. It's one thing for an Olympic Games to be in the red after the party's over. But before a single skater puts blade to ice?

For Mason's part, he was plainly tickled to have precipitated all this coverage with what he describes as "that nice, big, juicy scoop." He says, "It was a pretty big deal at the time because it was the first indication that the project was in serious trouble." And the problem was less the size of the loan than the fact that the City advanced it in secret, he says.

Asked now to look back on the decision and the election, Ladner just sounds tired. When the story broke, Ladner says, "I remember how frustrating it was: I couldn't talk about it without weakening the hand of the City. We were just backstopping the developer." He adds that the City's lawyer at the time advised that the City had made a legal commitment to build the village. It had to be done. The situation was made worse, Ladner says, because he liked and trusted the Maleks. "They were gracious and capable—good partners." CBC News reported Ladner's most memorable conclusion: "If necessary, I am prepared to lose this election to save this project and protect the city's taxpayers."

Lose he did.

Robertson, who had enjoyed such success in castigating Ladner and everyone else at the City for conducting all the high-dollar business meetings behind closed doors, took office and immediately convened a series of closed-door meetings, announcing at a December 9, 2008, news conference that he and his Vision councillors were "just making sure we restore public confidence in the project." The first public pronouncement came six weeks later, in January 2009, when the new mayor put out a news release, which didn't add any new information, but seemed calculated to continue piling blame on the previous administration: "The Olympic Village is a billion-dollar project, and the City's on the hook for all of it ... We now know why the previous city government didn't want to talk about the deal they'd made. The arrangements were not in the public's interest."

New Vision councillor Geoff Meggs, Robertson's hard-charging right-hand man, told a special meeting of council, "In my judgment, the city may face the largest financial loss in its history." By Meggs's telling, all signs were bad, and notwithstanding the willing participation of the Vision councillors of the day, the responsibility rested entirely on the NPA politicians and their administration supporters who had negotiated on the City's behalf. Robertson and company sacked city manager Judy Rogers, replacing her with the former provincial deputy health minister Penny Ballem. Deputy city manager Jody Andrews resigned soon after, which put Vancouver under new management. (Andrews is now Deputy City Manager in the Denver suburb of Westminster, Colorado.) The City was under new management.

In keeping with the tradition of Olympic overreach, Vancouver was exposed, reputationally as well as financially. The City was also limited in its options. The federal and provincial governments had both insisted loudly that they would not bail the City out. And while the previous Council had been able to find $100 million to finance a couple of months of construction, the City of Vancouver Charter restricted further spending from City reserves. But, amidst the economic calamity that was still unfolding from the subprime mortgage crisis, it was clear that Millennium wasn't going to get the money anywhere else.

So, with construction cranes threatening to stop swinging, Vancouver had to appeal to the Government of British Columbia to amend the Charter to allow the City to borrow enough to pay for future construction and, if necessary, to cover the project's accumulated debt to Fortress. The province passed that new legislation in a matter of weeks, and the City acted with equal alacrity, meeting with Fortress, paying out the accumulated $320-million debt and assuming the responsibility (and ultimately the profitability of) the high-interest loan to Millennium.

The Maleks got news of this change obliquely and unexpectedly. Jonathan Klein, managing director of Fortress Investments, rang Shahram to say that he had come to Vancouver and would like to meet for coffee at Fortress's usual haunt, the five-star Opus Hotel in

Yaletown. When Shahram arrived, Klein welcomed him to the bar where Dean Dakolias, one of Fortress's principals, was also waiting, and they immediately began to apologize. Klein said the City had taken over their loan, adding that he was now worried for the Maleks and was feeling bad that they had wound up in this position.

Shahram says now that it was awkward and embarrassing to learn of the change in circumstances from their former financiers. More than that, however, it was unsettling. Although always polite, the relationship with Fortress had never been warm. Beyond the difficult terms of the deal they had negotiated, the Maleks, in their old-world courtliness, had never meshed with the chain-smoking, often-profane hedge fund managers. And yet Klein and company had made a special trip to express their disappointment and pay their respects, which Shahram found touching. These were the people the Maleks had been facing in extremely tough negotiations, and now, "they were feeling sorry for *us!*" At that moment, it felt like there was much worse to come.

Sure enough, the walls began to push in from every direction. Just before the election and as one of the conditions to advancing the $100 million, the City had approached Millennium one more time, asking for a further injection of $25 million immediately and in cash. It was an unusual request for an additional demonstration of the Maleks' commitment, and their capacity to continue—although perhaps not that unusual. The City had requested a $29-million deposit in 2007, as a condition of Millennium being selected to build the Olympic Village.

That earlier payment had been a strong sign of commitment by Millennium, and a significant economic inconvenience, even in better times. Now, amid the banking lockdown that followed the 2008 crisis—as well as the intense public scrutiny on this increasingly politicized project—the Maleks knew they were going to have a more difficult time funding another $25 million, especially so quickly. But the City was both adamant and encouraging. In a final meeting before Judy Rogers and Jody Andrews were replaced by the new Vision Vancouver administration, Rogers said, "Just make this one last payment and you will see a very different City," the implication being that seeing that money, the Vancouver officials would be a great deal more supportive and accommodating. So the Maleks paid the additional $25 million, hoping it would be the last big ask, as they went about finishing the project.

But the promise of "a very different City" played out differently after Rogers and Andrews were pushed out of their positions. The Maleks remember how incoming city manager Penny Ballem suggested they step aside so she could install the CEO of a competing company as the new project lead. The Maleks strenuously declined that offer. As an alternative, Ballem insisted upon installing an observer to work out of Millennium's office and to oversee—and sometimes overrule—some of the day-to-day decisions that the Maleks or Hank Jasper would normally have made without hesitation, or second-guessing.

Word soon got out that Peter and Jasper—both formidable forces—were perhaps no longer the last avenue of appeal, and Millennium's contractors started dragging their feet or demanding and pushing back—acting both nervously and aggressively. The nervousness was understandable. Reading the newspaper coverage of the day, you might have thought that this was a controversial project in danger of collapse; the contractors would want to protect their own positions. But they also understood that the Maleks and the City had their backs to the wall. As Jasper had said, with the Olympics coming, there was no Plan B. So people started to push. For example, the contractors became more and more creative and insistent about identifying "extras"— that is, billing additionally for items they claimed weren't covered in the original contracts. And the City's observer seemed bent on getting in the way, signing off on cost increases.

Jasper says, "The observer was more concerned about the City's turnover schedule to VANOC than [Millennium's] cost and budget controls." This, Jasper goes on, "created an impossible and unacceptable situation for Millennium, where a lenders' representative, rather than support its borrower's attempts to control cost—as a lender would typically do—was acting instead as an advocate for the contractors," actively inflating the final price.

Put another way, a lender's representative—a professional banker—would normally be fiercely conservative, urging the developer to contain costs at every turn. The City's rep, on the other hand, consistently signed off on cost increases. On the design front, that might merely have been an effort to support the political priority of a greener development. Jasper and Peter both report that the observer also supported the City's constant requests for the previously mentioned and increasingly ambitious green building features, from window shades on the Erickson building to recycled flush-toilet water.

When it came to subcontractor requests, for more overtime or additional features, it's entirely likely that the City just didn't want to take any chances—or countenance any long arguments over the bills—when it was still worrying about hitting an Olympic deadline. But it left Millennium to manage the increasing expenses, and carry the costs of its steadily rising debt.

In an interview after the project concluded, Don Voth, then president of Metro-Can, the larger of two general contractors executing the work, said this must have been particularly painful for Peter, precisely because managing subcontractors and adjudicating change orders is something that he does extraordinarily well. Voth said that even among Vancouver's best developers, Peter has an unusually comprehensive understanding of construction and a prodigious work ethic. Even without the encouragement coming from the City, sub-contractors on a job this size would inevitably have argued to increase their billing by claiming extra work—and the developer would have to review every claim. At Olympic Village, Voth said, "we had thousands. We had whole binders of them, and Peter would just sit down for hours and grind through." And because Peter was known to be knowledgeable, tough, and fair, he was accustomed to settling every claim without ever triggering a dispute that would bring in the lawyers. But with the City constantly in the way, the process became egregiously difficult. Millennium did what it could to manage the overruns, but Peter says that he was frustrated that the City was both preventing him from doing his job and actively driving up his costs. As a result, he says, "the contractors made an absolute killing."

In the meantime, a group of buyers who had put down deposits in the pre-sale started legal action to try to cancel their purchase. They'd paid top dollar in a hot market and the condo values had dropped sharply—partly because of the general real estate crisis, and partly because the City's senior political leaders were constantly in the news describing the project as some kind of Olympic debacle. Sensing an opportunity to wriggle out of their contracts, and encouraged by some eager law firms that were soliciting participants for a potential class action lawsuit, the cold-footed buyers used Fortress's deficiency reports to argue that the work was substandard and that they should be excused from their commitments. The legal assault failed, but it contributed further to the public impression that this crown jewel of a project was never going to get done on time—or be worthy when it was finished.

To make matters worse, the City went to a consortium of Canadian banks to refinance the Fortress loan down to a reported flat 2.25 percent—great news! But to Millennium's surprise and intense disappointment, the City continued to charge Millennium the +/-10.5 percent rate that the New Yorkers had levied in the first place. According to a 2014 "City of Vancouver Backgrounder," this manoeuvre turned out to "save taxpayers an estimated $110 million." Put another way, the City extracted an extra $110 million from Millennium with a marked-up loan.

Ken Bayne says this was the juncture at which "the whole thing could have fallen apart. It was a huge distraction. But to Millennium's credit, they continued full bore."

Certainly, there were many people who might have suggested that Millennium bolt rather than continue to suffer the insults and economic risk. Having been pushed so hard by City Hall to deliver this prestige package against a crazy deadline—only to be slandered as incompetent—Hank Jasper says, "any other developer would have just tossed the City the keys and said, 'We'll see you in court.'" Michael Flanigan, then the City of Vancouver's director of real estate services and later vice president of development and asset management at BC Housing, agrees: "This had to be the most ambitious project in North America at the time. No one else in the sector could have built that many units at once; and any other developer would have walked." Even Amir Malek was questioning their compliance. As the City continued to push and push, Amir suggested that it might be time for his sons to dig in their heels, not to bail but to drive a harder bargain, even if they had to threaten to halt construction until they secured their position.

Peter and Hank were thinking along the same lines, questioning whether the politicians were acting in good faith. But Shahram was still remembering a different City of Vancouver, the one exemplified by Eric West, who had been so helpful when the brothers were just breaking into the Vancouver market. He was thinking about Michael

Flanigan's promise that "the City won't hurt you" and about Judy Rogers saying, "just make this one last payment and you will see a very different City." And he said to Peter and Hank, "If we finish on time, if we deliver this very special project, I am sure the City will appreciate all that we have done."

Even without the rose-coloured glasses, even in the face of an increasingly hostile and unhelpful municipal overseer, Peter says, "We couldn't fathom stopping. We just wanted to put our heads down and do the work." And so they did.

AMIDST ALL THIS drama, there was a perverse dividend. As the subprime crisis shuddered through the economy, crashing real estate prices, Roger Bayley says that other developers in the greater Vancouver region quickly hit the pause button on twenty major projects, freeing up an enormous number of tradespeople in what had been an overheated and critically competitive market. The bad news was that Millennium had already inked a lot of contracts and the prices were fixed, so they couldn't leverage the downturn to save money. "But," Bayley says, "it made a big difference to getting the work done. Had the [subprime] collapse not happened, the whole project might never have been finished on time."

When Peter first heard Bayley's take that the subprime collapse might have been the thing that saved the project, he was offended. Even if he is not as inclined as Shahram to always search for the good side in people and the good potential in every deal, Peter is still an optimist; he usually just shakes this stuff off. But it was clear in his demeanour that, despite his regard for Bayley and his appreciation for Bayley's contribution, this contention—the mere suggestion that Millennium would ever have failed—pushed him past the point of patience. These, after all, are people who would pour concrete against a serenade of gunfire rather than walk out on a deal. There was a point of principle here, and if it took every ounce of experience and professionalism, creativity, and budgetary bloody-mindedness, as far as both brothers were concerned, they were *never* going to miss that deadline.

A PROMISE KEPT

On the eve of the Winter Olympics' opening ceremonies, the waterfront condo complex in Vancouver that is housing more than 2,700 Olympic athletes and team officials is winning almost universal praise from its guests. The suites are, to borrow a favorite snowboarding phrase, sweet, with marble-top counters in the shiny new kitchens. Each unit has a living-room area—a far cry from the dormlike conditions of Villages past. And the views are nothing short of breathtaking. Many apartments look out onto an inlet and the silver downtown skyline, with snowcapped mountains as a backdrop. "It's blown us away, to be honest," says U.S. speedskater Chad Hedrick, who won gold, silver, and bronze medals at the 2006 Winter Olympics in Turin, Italy, and is a medal contender this year. "They really went big on this. It's a million-dollar view, for sure."

—*TIME* MAGAZINE, FEBRUARY 2010

This is part of the story that often slips beneath the radar: Olympic Village, which was built in record time, amid controversy, and under an unprecedented amount of pressure—was an outrageous success. That certainly is the view of Mark Cutler, the Australian consultant and big-games fixer who was the 2010 Olympic director of villages development. And yes, the plural is correct: villages—one on Southeast False Creek and another in Whistler, which was the site for most of the alpine events. Looking at the Vancouver example, he says, "It's up there with the very best of any Olympic village I have ever seen."

Cutler, a veteran of the 2000 Olympic Summer Games in Sydney, Australia, was the Vancouver Organizing Committee (VANOC) "employee number 17," joining the team in 2004. It was his job to liaise with the City of Vancouver, with Millennium, and with the architects and contractors to make sure that the far-sighted, sustainable, mixed-use new neighbourhood would, for two weeks, be a perfect party place for the world's foremost hardbodies. Cutler says, "I developed quite a good rapport with the Millennium team, and with the City of Vancouver. And"—he understates—"I know that there was some angst at times between the two. But my role was to be perpetually reminding them that one of the prizes in this would be getting an outcome in 2010 that would stand everybody in very good stead." Among all parties, he credits Shahram for his single-minded commitment "to making this a fantastic village experience for all of the Olympic athletes. That really struck a chord for me."

The actual circumstances of the project, Cutler describes as "a perfect storm." Even before the financial crisis, you had a tight schedule and a long list of often contradictory agendas—including the post-game demands and the untested sustainability features. Midway through construction, the International Olympic Committee (IOC) decided that the village would also be used for the Paralympic Games, extending by two more weeks the amount of time the project would be unavailable for completion or sale. Yet, each time Cutler went back to the Maleks with another wrinkle or another request, "I found them very reasonable. I found them gracious."

Aside from the obvious goal of actually finishing the buildings on time, there was a further complication of delivering them in appropriate condition. The accommodations had to be nice enough for the athletes, and robust enough to still look saleably new, even after a couple of weeks of hard use by a group of ebullient youngsters who might not be perfectly cautious about dragging their bags across new hardwood floors or keeping wet or scratchy gear off the marble countertops. The floors were an easy fix: Millennium carpeted everything and then pulled the carpet up when the Games were over. But the kitchens were a bigger challenge. First, Cutler says, the IOC wanted the athletes to eat in a single, central location, "bringing everybody from every nation together." Beyond the community-building agenda, "you can create housekeeping nightmares when you've got 80 or 100 different nationalities, different cultures, all deciding that they want to cook in someone's new oven—in their own way, in their own time, using their own menu ... and many athletes of the world are actually very young adults. And if they take it upon themselves to start operating some of those electrical appliances, who knows what might happen?" So, Millennium carefully erected interior plywood panelling to protect the custom German Eggersmann kitchens and the Sub-Zero and Miele appliances for the length of the Games.

When Millennium handed over the keys—a full one hundred days before the Olympics were to begin—VANOC president and CEO John Furlong celebrated the moment, saying, "I wish I was one of the athletes coming to the Games—to be able to be in those rooms and look out on that view. You can feel the magic that has been performed on this site."

There was a grand ceremony, with drummers from the Musqueam First Nation ushering Furlong and a cheerful Mayor Gregor Robertson into the beautifully refurbished Salt Building—soon to be the Athletes' Living Room. Robertson said, "We had some difficulties raising money, but progress of the construction has been smooth, and we are sincerely thankful to those concerned," though he didn't thank the Maleks, standing in the background. But he boasted about the sustainability elements that are so generously embedded in the project and said, "as these facilities come with all these features, they will be sold without any problem for general use after the Games."

Three days later, on November 7, 2009, there was another ceremony on-site, which marked the first time that His Royal Highness Prince Charles brought his new wife, Camilla, on a Royal Visit to Canada. The Maleks were honoured to be included and charmed by the royal couple, who Shahram said, "have a good sense of humour." The new Duchess of Cornwall and her Prince "were very easy to get on with." Any reservations people had about Millennium or the Olympic development seemed to have evaporated in a wave of goodwill that seemed to extend to the Maleks as well. Among Olympic planners and organizers, they were the toast of the town.

Three months later, when the athletes arrived, they too celebrated their luxurious digs. They raved about the creature comforts and conveniences of the village. They partied in the park and on the waterfront. Where other Olympic villages are generally austere and featureless dormitories, the Vancouver suites were beautiful, and the future commercial spaces meant there was room for a gym and workout and warm-up spaces, medical facilities, administrative facilities and cafés, in addition to the central mess hall, which were arrayed around a central plaza and park. It wasn't just a place to bunk down; it truly was a village.

Cutler says it became a running joke during the Games that VANOC officials were going to have to hire security to make the athletes leave—especially the Canadians, who were lapping up luxury in the Erickson-Milkovich waterfront condos—the veritable cherry among *Time* magazine's "sweet" suites. These were opulent apartments that would ultimately sell (even in a shaky market) for more than $4 million each, causing Cutler to wonder if the Canuck team's unprecedented medal haul was partly thanks to the inspiring surroundings. "It was such a fantastic facility," he says, "and in such a beautiful location."

As a bonus, for an Olympic village consultant who was working himself out of a job, Cutler also wound up conducting tours for an observer program, serving people who were planning for future Olympic games, in London and Sochi, and for other events, such as the 2015 Pan American Games that were then scheduled for Toronto. Cutler says: "I got three job offers, all on the basis, presumably, that I could assist them in getting some sort of comparable outcome."

Cutler stayed in Vancouver for four more years, working on several of those projects remotely. He is married to a Canadian and their two children were born during Cutler's time in Vancouver. In 2014, he took the whole brood back to Australia, where he had signed on to manage the village for the 2018 Commonwealth Games on the Gold Coast, south of Brisbane. He brought fresh eyes when the family came back to Vancouver for a visit later that year. They spent a day walking and cycling around Olympic Village and found "that it was reflecting exactly the city's ambition for the legacy of the Games. It was just a fantastically vibrant, mixed-use community with great amenities—well lived-in, buzzing, obviously with a lot of vibrancy ... and I thought: Well, okay, so there were challenges. But the City should be going: 'Look at this! This is exactly what we had envisaged.' I can't imagine that it wouldn't have met their expectations, if not exceeded them."

As to the Maleks, Cutler says, "They honoured their commitments, and that made the city look fantastic!"

Making the triumph complete, in the first week of the Games in 2010, the US Green Building Council (USGBC) identified the Olympic Village Neighbourhood as the first LEED Platinum-certified community, distinguishing it, by the standards of the day, as the greenest, most energy-efficient and sustainable neighbourhood on earth. While Mayor Robertson had been (and would continue to be) a trenchant critic of the development, he celebrated the honour at a news conference with the USGBC's Tim Cole, saying, "This should be a source of pride for residents and an example to the rest of the world. [This] is a big feather in our cap, as we move towards our goal of becoming the greenest city in the world by 2020."

Again, however, Robertson failed to invite the Maleks to share the honour, or to offer Millennium passing acknowledgment, a lack of graciousness that the brothers found more mysterious than annoying. In all the bruising meetings that had occurred in the run-up to the Games, in the financial arguments and interfering, Robertson had never been in the room. And when they bumped into one another on public occasions, they say that he was polite in a no-hard-feelings kind of way, but not engaged—positively or negatively.

No matter: for as long as the Games continued, the Maleks took quiet pleasure from their achievement and enjoyed their status as Olympic sponsors. Peter says that, notwithstanding the City's apparent Malek blackout policy, "We were treated like celebrities." They got to run with the Olympic flame, a privilege the brothers shared with Peter's eldest daughter Roxanna, then thirteen, and with Shahram's two sons Nader, sixteen, and Alex, fifteen. During the Games, they shared a bounty of tickets with family and friends (Shahram says, "Our parents were here the whole time!") and they entertained guests in the luxury box they were assigned at Rogers Arena, where Canada's team clinched the Gold Medal hockey game.

"It was such a great time for Vancouver," Shahram says, "and it was fun for us after a gruelling thirty months." Peter says, "Yeah, it was fun." But, he adds, darkly, "It's good that we didn't know what was going to happen."

DECONSTRUCTION

In the spring of 2010, there was a warm glow in the streets of Vancouver. There was still some tallying to do, there was some climate-change-related head shaking about how much snow Olympic organizers had been forced to make to stage the mountain events. There was some lingering horror about the death of a twenty-one-year-old luge competitor. But, for the most part, the 2010 Winter Olympics had been a fantastic party and a global success. Everyone had done their best work, had finished on time, and had basked in superlative reviews from the world press. The naysayers had grown silent. Mostly.

In a battered international real estate climate, the rushed timing of Millennium's gargantuan project was also starting to look like luck. While most players in the residential development business had paused after the 2008 crash, Millennium had continued and was now in a position to come to market with a spectacular new community that was still emanating Olympian goodwill. The prices had already bounced back beyond their pre-2008 highs. Things were looking up.

Or maybe not. The City's continuing criticism of the project and the lawsuits from buyers unhappy to have paid an early premium had left a toxic sheen on the Olympic Village product—and on the village itself. In the words of the planner, developer, and constant critic Michael Geller, it was a "ghost town." People were slow to buy because they kept reading claims of trouble with construction, and hearing direct criticism from a Vision Vancouver council that never stopped treating the Village like a poisoned holdover from their political rivals. The City, which—remember—had bought out the Fortress position to become the sole lender, convened a news conference to complain about deficiencies in the project, inviting reporters into a suite that had been damaged when a toilet overflowed from a unit above. This was not indicative of the construction standard, but it certainly had the capacity to erode public confidence in the development (and the developer) and hamper the marketability of the other units. (It seems fair to say that no for-profit financial institution would call a press conference to trash a project on which they held the only mortgage.)

The slow sales contributed to the classic chicken-and-egg dilemma that arises when you're trying to bring a "complete community" onto the market: businesses don't want to move into a new neighbourhood until there are enough people to support their operation, and the people don't want to move in until fundamental services are already in place. As the City of Vancouver's then-director of real estate services Michael Flanigan puts it, "No stores, no people; no people, no stores." However, the Maleks were confident that the impressive array of anchor tenants they had already signed up (Urban Fare, London Drugs, TD Bank, Legacy Liquor, and others) would make Olympic Village the vibrant, self-sustained community they had promised.

For all his criticism, Geller says he has long admired the Maleks. He says that their City-in-the-Park development in Burnaby was "not just a series of buildings, but a real community." He also worked with them directly in the early 2000s when he was the CEO of SFU Community Trust, which was then beginning the development of UniverCity, the now-complete community adjacent to the Simon Fraser University campus on top of Burnaby Mountain. Millennium built the first condo project on the mountain, One University Crescent, and Geller says it remains one of the best developments at UniverCity and one of the most creative in the region. He says, "My one regret is that I didn't buy one of the units."

Geller, who as the original planner for Granville Island, remains emotionally invested in the neighbourhood, was also one of the people who argued for a low-rise approach in Southeast False Creek, and he was hopeful about the Maleks' involvement. He says, "They do very special, very high-quality projects, and they bring an international perspective; they are truly citizens of the world." But Geller had criticized the City's demands on the Olympic Village site from the outset: he said the streets were too narrow and the population too dense, and it included an impractical and, he insisted, unaffordable number of low-income units. He also told anyone who wanted to hear it—and everyone else besides—that the City of Vancouver's close involvement added too much risk.

Time proved Geller right about a few things and wrong about others. Narrow streets are an increasingly popular, pedestrian-friendly feature in any walkable community, and as on the north shore of False Creek, the population density has proved an attractive feature. Look at the development today on any nice day and you can see even more people flocking to enjoy the neighbourhood and the shops and services that can only survive in a dense urban environment. As for the affordable housing, it's all but indistinguishable because of the consistent quality of construction; it fits perfectly well. Of course, Geller was right about the political risk, but it turned out that everyone apart from the Maleks did well financially. Indeed, at a time when other construction projects were shuttering all over the region, Millennium's leading contractors and all of their subs enjoyed continuing work and, in many cases, unprecedented profits, supported by the City's overreach.

Thanks to his stream of criticism in newspaper columns and radio commentaries, Geller also gets blamed for helping to undermine the value of the project in the immediate post-Olympic period. But he's indignant at that notion, saying that he was observing a problem, not causing it. "The City completely mismanaged it," he says. For example, he points out that the City dragged its feet in finding an operator to manage the affordable rental product it had commissioned Millennium to build—370 units of non-market housing the City had insisted be included in the project. In failing to fill those units promptly, or even bothering to put them on the market, the City actually obstructed the kind of population bump that would have helped bring life to the village. Geller says the City also acted belligerently in even the most mundane matters. He recalls a faded sign posted on the front door of the presentation centre that said, "Don't park on the street or the police will tow your car." In a neighbourhood where the biggest problem was the *lack* of traffic, Geller says, the City had surrounded the sales centre with No Parking signs, looking all the more like it was trying to block the development's success.

The discouraging signage notwithstanding, the Maleks calmly moved on to the ambitious sales campaign that was necessary to fill a massive project that, until this point in the summer of 2010, they had been forced to keep empty in the public interest. Bob Rennie's sales team started strong. Phil Chung joined the team in May 2010 thinking, "Who wouldn't want to be part of the Olympic Village legacy?" Twenty agents began a weeklong training session featuring speakers from Millennium and walk-throughs of all the available buildings. Construction manager Hank Jasper gave a detailed presentation on everything from the sustainability features to the finer points of the landscaping. Chung says, "There was so much to know." Rennie's "hoopla launch" brought in huge crowds, with people lining up to see seven suites that had been prepared and furnished by some of Vancouver's top interior designers and furniture showrooms, including Robert Ledingham, Mitchell Freedland, Inform Interiors, The Cross, and William Switzer. Rennie says now that some of the traffic included people who were basically tourists in their own town, out to get a closer look at the Olympic lodgings and to snap up "passports" that they could get stamped and submit later for a prize. But, as both Rennie and the Maleks point out, these were also the kinds of visitors who would help generate buzz. Given the post-crash timing and the sheer volume of product, the Maleks expected the campaign to ramp up over many months—certainly not to sell out in the first week. The City's impatience, like its obstructionism, was counterproductive, Shahram says, adding "It was an excellent campaign. It just needed a little time."

Given the project's profile, there were also some other odd political interruptions. On one mid-summer Thursday, a colleague asked Chung to stay late to look after a young couple who had been scouting a pricey two-bedroom suite for their father, who was supposed to be flying in from Calgary. Chung remembers that they were late arriving ("I had to cancel my boot camp") and that he was surprised there were five people in the party—introduced as the father, his son and daughter, and their respective partners. He also remembers there was a ruckus on the street, a small group of housing activists who seemed to be starting some kind of rally outside the community centre. No matter, Chung led the party to the building and let them into the suite.

Not long into the visit, the father pulled Chung aside and said he was not feeling well and had to go get some medication from his car. "Let's not alarm the kids," he added. He and Chung slipped out together; the building was still locked up, Chung had to buzz him out.

Chung returned to the apartment in a matter of minutes and was surprised to find the door locked. "I remember stepping back and looking around to be sure I was on the right floor." He was, so he took out his master key and let himself in, picking up what he thought was a flyer off the floor as he walked through the entrance hall. When he got to the living room, he found the four young people all sitting in a circle on the floor, exhibiting "a completely different demeanour."

Chung continues: "The lead guy pulled out a script and started reading, 'We are the people of...'" Chung says now that he can't even remember the cause, but he clearly recalls that the leader announced that he and his mates were now having a sit-in. They had also unfurled a banner and hung it from the balcony. It read, "False Creek False Promises," and while they never got to expound upon their own particular grievances, it was clear from a cheering group of nearly sixty protesters on the street that they were hitting a nerve.

Chung spent years working in hotel operations before switching to real estate. "I've closed down a few parties in my time. So, I put on my hotel hat and asked them to leave. When they refused, Chung called the sales office and reported that he was being held by activists, at which point, the leader said, "You can leave. This is a peaceful demonstration."

Chung stayed, and was soon joined by Rennie's sales manager, Yvonne Dawson, her daughter, two construction workers, and a distinctly unamused Peter Malek. Chung recalls, "He was upset!" When

Dawson picked up the flyer that had been on the floor, she found that it was actually some kind of manifesto. But when she began to read it, Peter took it and started tearing it up. By the time the police arrived, their biggest challenge was not getting the protesters to leave, but convincing Peter not to press charges.

Peter recalls the story with a shrug and a smile, saying, "it was not much of a hostage taking." The protesters were quickly outnumbered and outmatched. But it became something of a marker for that summer—a reminder that if something *could* go wrong, it would.

As fall approached, it became increasingly obvious that the City had no intention of becoming suddenly supportive of the project, which Michael Flanigan says was a political rather than bureaucratic decision: "For Vision, it had been a brilliant political strategy." Mayor Gregor Robertson and his caucus had got elected "by blowing up the Village. How could they go back and be buddy with the developer?"

As the director of real estate services, Flanigan with his team tracked prices of all real estate in Vancouver proper and the extended Metro region. It was clear from that analysis that "Olympic Village had fallen under a cloud of controversy of our own making." Flanigan says, "Had the politicians not soured the project, the Millennium campaign would have reached $1,100 or $1,200 per square foot," a price that was comparable to what new high-end product was selling for across False Creek, and one that would have well justified the original $190-million purchase price for the land.

At this point, however, the Maleks were appealing to the City as lender to allow them to reduce the prices far enough and for long enough to get the product moving, to overcome the post-Olympic "ghost town" image and generate some buzz. But the City refused, insisting that the Maleks would need full price to completely pay out the City loan.

Conscious that they had payments to make, the Maleks next proposed bulk selling some of the units to willing investors. It was highly likely that a deep-pocketed investor would be happy to pick up a tranche of this kind of quality product and sit on it for a few years, riding the prices back up. As Michael Geller and Roger Bayley both noted at the time, the project was held in much higher regard around the world than it was in Vancouver. Again, the City said no—and as both regulator and lender, it was firmly in the driver's seat. The only way it would agree to adjust the terms was if Millennium put up even more security to guarantee the City's ultimate income. And, by this point, there was really no room for the Maleks to do so in such a short time.

As the weeks passed, things were looking dark, figuratively and literally. As Phil Chung points out, if you're selling a big project like this—or even just a single building with some extremely high-end, high-price units on the higher floors—it's industry practice to sell the least-expensive product first. Then, as the project begins to sell out, the remaining units become even more exclusive. It's in those last, big-dollar sales where developers make most of their money—and where the Maleks had planned to recover any shortfall had the City let them prime the market with some quick, lower-cost sales to create momentum in their marketing campaign. So, Rennie's team had been concentrating sales along the interior streets, preserving everything that was facing the water. This meant that people looking at the village from across False Creek saw only the empty waterfront buildings that were dead in the daytime, dark at night. While there was gathering energy within the development, most people saw only the quiet fringe and the ghost-town stories they were reading in the papers.

The brothers expected a slow start. They knew their marketing strategy would take time to take effect. But there might have been a moment, in October 2010, when they hoped that people had finally started to recognize and give credit for what they had achieved. The upturn in tone came from a *Vancouver Sun* article written by Rob Macdonald, who was every kind of insider: the president of Macdonald Development Corporation; a director of the Urban Development Institute; and a former member of a blue-ribbon group that Mayor Robertson had assembled the previous year to review the Olympic Village deal. Macdonald wrote, in blunt terms, that most of the problems with the development were of the City's own making. Having committed to building out Southeast False Creek as an Olympic project, he said, the City had started slowly and then piled too many costs and expectations on the developer. The City forced Millennium to absorb the cost of site cleanup, demanded unprecedented sustainability standards, and then structured the land deal in a way that, as it had been warned, could never be financed. And when it stepped in, to scoop the project from the Fortress melt-down, the City kept the predatory interest rates, notwithstanding its much lower costs. It made no consideration for the overtime-driven price inflation caused by the foreshortened and inflexible construc-tion schedule, nor for the enforced break in the sales campaign. Olympic security concerns meant Millennium had to shut down all sales, Macdonald wrote, "just when a world of customers had come to visit."

To cap it all off, he said, "Some people at City Hall have been saying things about the development that have substantially damaged the project's salability and brand reputation—something that no sensi-ble lender would do."

Pleading with the City to "get all inexperienced hands off the tiller," Macdonald closed with this:

Millennium Water is one of the finest environmentally conscious projects ever built. It is located in a beautiful spot in one of the world's greatest cities. It will prove to be a tremendous success in the long run. All it needs is experienced calm hands to guide it through the selling stage. Peter and Shahram Malek are decent, award-winning developers. They deserve to be treated with respect and handed a silver medal for delivering the project on time for the Olympics despite all the difficulties they faced.

Peter and Shahram celebrated the piece when it appeared and they still cherish it today because it was well researched and totally unexpected. It was an unsolicited endorsement, courageous and factual, and all the more poignant because it was coming from another successful developer.

In another nicely redemptive moment around the same time, Scot Hein, the City's senior urban designer, was invited to Chicago for LivCom, the International Awards for Livable Communities, sponsored by the United Nations Environment Programme. Olympic Village was a finalist among entries from twenty-six countries—and in the Olympic spirit, Vancouver took gold. But when Hein returned with the hardware, excited to share the news with a mayor who had carved out an international reputation for his initiative to distinguish Vancouver as the greenest city in the world, Gregor Robertson and company appeared distinctly uninterested. In an interview ten years later, Hein said, "I don't think there's been a press release about that award, yet. That really hurt the Maleks."

"TO US IT felt like an ambush."

Even now, a decade later, Shahram seems bruised as he speaks those words. He and Peter had been summoned in November 2010 to meet with city manager Penny Ballem and her team. And here it might be worth noting that, when Rob Macdonald referred to "inexperienced hands" at City Hall, and given the criticism from journalists and commentators at the time, the shot seemed to be aimed at Ballem. City manager from 2008 to 2015, Ballem is a medical doctor, a former university professor, and, before taking the City position, had quit her job as the provincial deputy minister of health after a public spat with then-premier Gordon Campbell over his approach to health care. Imperious and renowned for micromanagement, she was a sharp change from her predecessor at City Hall, Judy Rogers, a widely admired delegator. Whereas, in the words of *Globe and Mail* municipal affairs writer and Langara University journalism professor Frances Bula, "Penny wanted to drive the tractor in the Pride parade. She believed she was way smarter than everybody and had to rescue everything." But of course, the other thing people agree upon is that Ballem really is, as Bula says, "way smarter" than most folks, which can be its own kind of blindness. If a brilliant person decides to accept advice only from people who are smarter still, they don't get a lot of practice listening. And even the smartest people can get themselves into trouble when working outside their field of expertise. Responding at the time to a Frances Bula report on a 2011 news conference in which Ballem was offering project updates, Michael Geller wrote, "Having just heard Dr. Penny Ballem explain OV [Olympic Village] finances on CBC, all I can say is I promise not to perform any medical procedures if she'll promise not to do any more real estate developments." He continues to complain today that Ballem didn't take the deal.

The Maleks' relationship with Ballem was also less than warm. From the moment in December 2008 that Vision Vancouver appointed her city manager, Peter says, she was "clinically efficient"—making clear that he was implying resolute heavy-handedness more than anything that actually improved the efficiency of their operation. The antipathy was never stated in an explicitly political way. No one at the City ever said to the Maleks' faces, "We don't want you here; we want to sever all links that might show the [previous] NPA [administration] was right to put their faith in your proposal." But in the first meeting with Ballem and other City staffers after the new administration took over, the brothers both remember Morley Koffman, one of the lawyers the City had engaged to advise on the action, telling them, "You are here at our sufferance."

Peter says, "It was chilling."

Still, by the time the Olympics were finished, the Maleks were not overly concerned about their ability to sell the units and make good on the loan. They had built something spectacular, against the clock, and the world had applauded. Yes, the product was moving slowly, but they had come up only $8 million short on their first $200-million, high-interest loan repayment in October 2010, an excellent result in the circumstances, and they had advised the City that they needed to work together to now reap the benefits of all the past work. Shahram says, "We were hoping for something reasonable. We expected to be negotiating a modification to the old Fortress loan to make it a win for everyone." It would have been easy, they thought, especially given how much less the City was now paying in interest on the outstanding amount than what they were charging Millennium.

Then, on October 7, 2010, the City—some would say with coldhearted efficiency—put a $1-billion charge on each of Millennium's other corporate projects and properties. The reaction of Millennium's lenders on those projects—including Evelyn, a development underway in West Vancouver at the time—was, as can be imagined, tantamount to panic.

The City showed no emotion about the utter havoc created in this way. It was a shock and a considerable blow, but the number seemed fanciful. Notwithstanding its headline potential, the City had never been at risk for anything near that amount, and now that the project was complete, there was no chance, even in a soft market, that Millennium or the City would be left with a deficit that was, in the worst case, anything but a small fraction of $1 billion.

The Maleks had also engaged PricewaterhouseCoopers (PwC), which was liaising with the City's accountants at Ernst & Young (EY), and the brothers remained optimistic that a deal was possible—and perhaps in the offing.

But when the brothers sat down on that November day with the City's team, there was no negotiation. As Shahram remembers it, "They basically said, 'It's nothing personal, but we're just going to put the project into receivership and take everything from you. If you don't agree, we will do it anyway.'"

The takeover of the completed Olympic Village was thereafter presented as a mutual decision. In a story in the *Globe and Mail,* Frances Bula said, "The city issued a statement late on Wednesday [November 16, 2010] in which the mayor praised the Maleks, whose company built the village. The brothers made equally gracious statements."

It was a bitter blow, the ultimate humiliation, Peter says. "If we had been dealing with a private lender, we would have been less trusting." He and Shahram were still thinking about the people at Vancouver City Hall who had helped them over the years, and still expecting something close to that level of support. But they had it exactly backwards. "A big bank or lender would never have called a loan when the project was already complete," Peter says. On the contrary, a bank would have been happy to extend more time on an investment that was clearly secure in the long term, and at a rate well above market.

But the City wasn't behaving like a creditor who might have to convince shareholders that a particular loan would be repaid in full (and with more accumulated interest) over a longer period of time. Rather, it looked like it was cleaning house on a potential political liability in the municipal election coming up the next year. Peter says, "They were just totally and utterly ruthless."

Penny Ballem declined an invitation to tell her side of the story. But the "nothing personal" sentiment rings through in comments from many of those involved—at least those who weren't at risk of losing their homes during the negotiations. Ken Bayne, the City's director of financial management and treasury, is pointedly complimentary of the brothers. He says, "They worked hard to deliver a quality project. They understood that they were doing something important for the City. And they were hung out in public for problems not of their making. But it was clear that Millennium was not going to be able to complete in the way the loan agreement was structured. Our view was that it was best for everyone if we just took over."

Michael Flanigan says again that the City itself was a big contributor to the development's troubles. "Gregor was a great guy and a great boss, but there was clearly some political opportunism." Vision Vancouver's critical position had turned into what Flanigan described as "a negative vortex," and "when Millennium was short on the loan, we had no choice but to step in and take over." As for the move to receivership being mutual, Flanigan says, "The legal agreements were so tightly woven in favour of the City that Millennium had no choice." The whole affair could well have wound up in court for a decade, but "Shahram and Peter took the high road—with dignity, integrity and stalwartness."

Though they are still choking over Ken Bayne's contention that this result was "best for everyone," the brothers are a great deal more at peace with Flanigan's interpretation. They thought about digging in. They considered how much they might improve their bargaining position if they took the City to court, even playing what the lawyers thought was a weak hand due to the trust they had placed in the City. But they decided, after a project that they still consider an unblemished success, that they didn't want to tarnish that legacy with a tawdry legal dispute. The high road looked like a better choice.

So, by triggering the receivership, the City was able to direct its lawyers to pick through the fine print of its agreement with Millennium and seize every piece of property the Maleks had pledged as security, a list that Flanigan says included "trophy properties," such as The Province Building that the Maleks had so lovingly restored. Within years, those were worth hundreds of millions of dollars. Even at the time, the brothers say the properties were worth much more than the disappointing amounts the City accepted in sales, liquidating the security that the Maleks could have used to underwrite their future business dealings.

To get a full sense of the City's appetite, when they noticed that Shahram and Peter's houses were still formally registered to their parents, Peter says the City's lawyers told them, "We have a fiduciary duty to write to your father to allow us to take the houses." Amir judged that he had a familial duty to refuse, and Peter and Shahram stayed in their homes.

Keeping their houses didn't feel like much of a consolation the day they walked into the Farris boardroom, their remaining assets hanging like so much easily picked fruit in those neatly arranged yellow file folders. In that moment, they weren't just being called to forfeit their fortune; they were being forced to actively sign it away. In the moment, it felt like a final act of defenestrating violence.

Still, it didn't end. In addition to seizing the actual properties, the City reached beyond. In one of the final sessions, when the City team was building the list of properties it was planning to extract, Shahram mentioned that Millennium had paid an option price of more than $3 million for a large block bounded by Columbia and Cook streets, between First and Second avenues—the site of the "No Parking" zone where the City had held Millennium's Olympic Village sales office hostage. The property sits kitty-corner off the southwest tip of the village itself, and the Maleks had planned to continue their neighbourhood building with a tall, curved tower that would fit nicely on the corner and complement the Village architecture perfectly. Without giving it much thought, Shahram said, "I hope you're not going to take that." There was no transferable value in that option; by its terms, the City couldn't resell it to recover more money. But Peter and Shahram both recall that Penny Ballem said that finding additional value for the City at this juncture wasn't the point. Rather, she said, it just wouldn't look good if Millennium continued building around Olympic Village, as if they had made off with some manner of profit from a development the City had dismissed as a complete economic failure. Peter says, "She told us it would be best if we find employment as consultants," selling their expertise to other developers.

Just to make the cleansing complete, the City also went around to all the buildings and edited out the Millennium branding. From the outset, the Maleks had called the development "Millennium Water," a name that was inscribed in handsome plaques in every major entryway. City crews searched out each of those plaques and covered them with a stick-on plastic cover that said: "The Village on False Creek." If you wander the neighbourhood today, you can see that many of the original plaques have re-emerged, as residents have scratched off the deteriorating plastic to reveal the higher-quality nameplates.

If it was expensive—and pointless—to walk away from the Columbia Street option, a bigger and more painful sacrifice came on the North Shore on a project that was not among the properties offered as security and was physically beyond the City of Vancouver's jurisdiction, but well within its sphere of influence. Millennium had been working for seven years on a land assembly above the Park Royal Shopping Centre in West Vancouver. They had purchased fifty-seven houses, an assembly that was outside the assets the City of Vancouver had seized, and they had gone through three rigorous and sometimes-controversial planning and rezoning exercises with the neighbours and with the District of West Vancouver council for a $500-million master planned community.

This was all rooted in a storied piece of land. A group of international investors, led by the stout-brewing Guinness family, had bought this property in 1931 as part of a 4,000-acre acquisition on what was then an isolated north shore—a slow ferry ride from the young city of Vancouver. The owners of these "British Pacific Properties" had big plans. They hired Olmsted Brothers, the firm that had designed Central Park in New York, to lay out the first 1,000-acre development on the upper slopes, a neighbourhood that is still known as British Properties. In the mid-1930s, they commissioned the Lions Gate Bridge, which opened in 1938 and changed the face of the North Shore forever. After the Second World War, they opened up two neighbourhoods closer to the bridge and called them Evelyn (named for a Guinness family daughter) and Almondel; they followed, in 1950, with Canada's first covered shopping mall: Park Royal.

In the early 2000s, the aging homes in Evelyn were worth barely as much as the extraordinary land on which they sat, and many of the homeowners started thinking they could gain more value by selling together than by moving out one by one. In 2003, a local real estate agent by the name of Barry McClure of Sutton Group had called Shahram and said that he was in touch with a majority of landowners in the enclave who had asked him to find an experienced developer to assemble and buy their properties for redevelopment, something that had been attempted in the past without success. So, Millennium embarked on this process cautiously, and at the request of the agent, the Maleks met Dan Pekovich, the lead landowner. Shahram was touched by Dan's sincerity and the detailed plan he had in mind for buying his family's and his neighbours' properties. But after assembling a large number of the houses and seeing that they were meeting resistance from remaining property owners, Millennium backed away.

Some weeks later, Shahram received a phone call at the office from a lady who in a crisp English accent said, "Mr. Malek, I am a property owner at Evelyn Drive, and your competition is assembling properties from the other end of Evelyn Drive and we don't like them. Are you going to do something about it?" It was enough to bring Millennium back into the picture.

The property is convenient and beautiful, boasting unobstructed views over First Narrows to Stanley Park—which is what caused the original commotion over the Maleks' involvement. While the majority of owners on the south side of Keith Road were keen to do a deal, those on the north side, who would not be part of the development, but whose views might be affected, rejected every option that Millennium proposed to build on the site below. Millennium engaged Arthur Erickson, whose global reputation was based partly on his success over the years in finding brilliant solutions for sloping sites. They offered Erickson and his talented associate Nick Milkovich the commission during a meeting at the Park Royal Caffe Artigiano, an occasion that Shahram says would have been memorable even if the Australian actor Hugh Jackman hadn't been sitting at the next table.

Still, northside residents—angry at the prospect of losing their views, and of living in a denser neighbourhood—pushed back, until West

Vancouver agreed with Shahram's suggestion to engage the former City of Vancouver director of planning Ray Spaxman (ultimately at Millennium's expense) to break the logjam. Spaxman, a revered elder in the regional planning community, and a nearby neighbour, led a planning exercise that included three people from the neighbourhood, one from the Park Royal Shopping Centre to the south, and Shahram on behalf of Millennium. And they finally came up with a master plan for a complete neighbourhood development that northside neighbours accepted—begrudgingly—because no part of it rises more than 2 storeys above Keith Road. The Maleks called the new project Evelyn to honour the original development and proposed to the municipality that a major street there be named Arthur Erickson Place to acknowledge the architect's role both in the project and in West Vancouver's modernist movement. They then built an appropriately luxurious sales centre on Taylor Way, preparing to launch what was to be a signature Millennium project.

Evelyn is a perfect case study of why the development industry is so complicated and so risky. There are so many moving parts. First, you have to assemble the land, negotiating with sellers, at least some of whom are sure to demand outrageous prices as soon as they realize their property is critical to a big and ambitious project. Then you have to assuage the concerns of nervous neighbours, of local First Nations groups, and of every department at the local municipality—transportation, services, recreation, parks, even the local school board. And if you happen to be in a neighbourhood where the nearby residents or business owners might be politically influential (which is to say, just about anywhere in tony West Vancouver), the stakes and the anticipated prices can rise astronomically. As in this case, the process can take many years, during which you wind up spending millions on consultants, planners, architects, and engineers—not to mention the costs of buying and holding the trove of pricey properties. And no part of this investment is secure until you tie down the last approval, round up the financing, build out the project, and, finally, sell the last homes. Only then can you be sure that the whole plan was profitable. And while an experienced developer can usually manage risk along the way, you're always conscious that, at any minute, the whole thing can come to a crashingly expensive halt.

Which is what happened at Evelyn. Notwithstanding the care, the attention, and the quality of work to date; notwithstanding the elegant projects for which Millennium was deservedly renowned in West Vancouver; notwithstanding decades of success in the region and beyond—in the post-Olympic chill, the people who had previously been on board to finance construction started backing slowly away. Indeed, a lender that had previously committed to supporting the project told the Maleks directly that the City of Vancouver had poisoned the deal, intervening to point out that it had seized all of the Maleks' security and was urging that funding be withheld. The Maleks suspected that it was, again, a question of optics. They felt stalked, as if it wasn't enough for the City of Vancouver to keep Millennium from working across the street from Olympic Village: the City didn't want to see them flourishing anywhere in the region.

One person deserves special mention here. Ralph Sultan, MLA for West Vancouver-Capilano, was a breath of fresh air. Ralph, who, among his many accomplishments, holds BASc, MBA, MA, PhD, and PEng academic designations and was a former Harvard professor, was wise and smart. At Shahram's request, he helped when Millennium hit a literal roadblock with 9th Street, a piece of unused road in Evelyn belonging to the Province. Its ownership and jurisdiction had delayed the project by a further sixteen months after the Spaxman report and was threatening to derail the entire development. Ralph brought the Province, the District of West Vancouver, the First Nations, and Millennium together in a room until an agreement was reached for Millennium to buy and to close the road. He showed remarkable courage: he knew what Millennium had gone through to obtain the rezoning and thought that all parties should work with Millennium. And he selflessly flew to Victoria with Shahram to help calm a lender during the prolific politicizing newspaper coverage during the Olympic Village project. Ralph exemplifies everything good about Canada and showed the decent side of Canadian politics.

It soon became obvious that the only way to save the development was by making the painful decision to relinquish it, allowing a competitor to pick up the property, enriched by the millions of dollars Millennium had spent on the planning and regulatory approvals. And true to the Maleks' vision, it turned out beautifully, just as they'd planned it. Most developers who take over a project midstream will make enough changes to suggest that they have somehow rescued a project. They'll shuffle something, add something, or take something away—doing enough, one way or another, to put their stamp on it. At the very least, they will change the name. But pretty much every detail of the Evelyn remained, a competitor's endorsement of the quality of the Maleks' work. The tall, curved tower that now sits kitty-corner from Olympic Village also looks a lot like the one that Millennium had planned before the City pushed them off the lot. Even when things were going wrong, it's clear that—in their vision and practice—the Maleks were still doing something right.

SOON AFTER THE City of Vancouver seized the project, sales in Olympic Village started to pick up. Having blocked Millennium from discounting prices, the City gave Rennie free rein to do what he thought was necessary to invigorate the market—which is to say: to act on the very advice that he, as Millennium's marketing consultant, had been giving all along. In February 2011, Rennie relaunched the sales campaign with prices slashed an average of 30 percent. He told the *Globe and Mail*, "Whether the city makes or loses money has no bearing; we just have to pay attention to stabilizing the asset for the taxpayer and maximizing revenue," a practical-sounding change from the City's previous position. Rennie boasted that in the previous ten days, he had received thirty-one offers on the 230 units then up for sale. In the same story, City councillor Geoff Meggs, Mayor Robertson's right hand, took no responsibility for the new approach. He said, "These decisions are now done by the receiver [Ernst & Young] with expert advice and the maximum value that those experts feel they can generate will flow back to taxpayers ... I think that it's a sophisticated approach and we'll see how the market responds."

Of course, the market might have responded more favourably had the City not declared the village to be an economic disaster zone by pushing the project into receivership. Now, even as prices were buoyant elsewhere in town, hard-core bargain hunters from around the region were sniffing around Olympic Village like urban coyotes stalking an injured cat.

The Maleks continued to anguish over the state of a project they still considered "theirs," and continued to work in the background for its success. Despite (or maybe because of) the presence of a sheath of signed leases, the City seemed slow to grasp the importance of keeping the anchor tenants like London Drugs and Urban Fare. At a time when the viability of the neighbourhood seemed to hang in the balance, it would have been a disaster had one or both of the majors tried to pull away. Beyond identifying these retail leaders in the first place, Millennium had redesigned the project extensively to accommodate their needs. Both London Drugs and Urban Fare have huge loading requirements: they need room for a procession of large trucks that bring everything from huge televisions to daily supplies of fresh foods. Having gone to the extreme of actually raising a building to make way for these essential community services, Shahram says he was shocked—and deeply concerned—when he heard the deals might be falling apart. So, while he was no longer responsible, he called Michael Flanigan in the City's real estate office and urged him to do everything possible to keep those tenants in place for the future vitality of the Olympic Village neighbourhood.

That campaign succeeded, and during the following months, the businesses set up shop, condo sales increased, and the village took on the life that the Maleks, and presumably the City, had expected. And by April 2014, a few months before the subsequent municipal election, Mayor Robertson took a sharp turn to the positive and announced that Olympic Village was a success after all. *Vancouver Sun* City Hall reporter Jeff Lee flagged his suspicions about the mayor's motivations in an April 28 story, titled, "In Olympic Village Debt Being Paid Off, Vancouver Politics Is Alive and Well." Lee went on to write, "Another sign that politicians are in full campaign mode for November's municipal election: on Monday the city announced it had finally sold the last remaining units in the Olympic Village."

The City's news release was singularly positive: "Final sale of Olympic Village wins gold for Vancouver taxpayers." The release announced that the City had "officially paid down the entire $630 million debt of the Olympic Village development, as well as recovered an additional $70 million." It had done so by "obtaining very low interest rates for the City's borrowed funds used to finance the Village" and then up-charging the Maleks on the debt, by selling the market rental buildings and the commercial strata space, by seizing and liquidating the Maleks' security, and by bulk-selling the last sixty-seven units to the Vancouver-based Aquilini Group for $91 million—the latter being an option that the City had specifically denied to Millennium.

It's interesting that the settlement amount, $630 million, was considerably below the $750-million credit line that the Maleks had originally negotiated with Fortress and 60 percent of the hysteria-level liability of $1 billion that Mayor Robertson and Councillor Meggs had mentioned in a January 2009 news conference. In 2014, there was only backslapping—for everyone except the Maleks. Robertson seemed to forget that he'd been prominent among the project detractors, now saying in the release, "There were many critics who said this would not happen, and that taxpayers would be left with a big debt." Aquilini Group president Francesco Aquilini, who had just scooped sixty-seven units that were rapidly rising in value, praised the project and the politicians who had so often stood in its way, saying, "Mayor Robertson and Vancouver City Council have helped finance a vibrant community that is now one of the most popular places to live in Vancouver."

The City news release was equally magnanimous in dispensing credit: "The current success of the Village was made possible by the combined efforts of: The Receiver, Ernst & Young ... and Rennie Marketing Systems..." Ernst & Young's senior vice-president, Kevin Brennan—whose firm had billed the City more than $5 million for services that Millennium would have performed as a cost of doing business—handed the credit right back, saying, "The City has worked hard to ensure all the debt from the Olympic Village development was fully paid back and that taxpayers are protected."

However, there remained a group of critics who were skeptical that the City had ever been at greater risk or that its intervention was timely or, ultimately, as profitable as the politicians were saying. For example, in a 2014 retrospective published in the *Georgia Straight*, veteran receivership expert David Bowra said, "I think you will discover that in all likelihood, the benefits were far fewer than the cost. I mean, the project was finished."

Comparing what happened in this political fishbowl to what was common practice, Bowra said: "I can assure you, in the almost 40 years that I've been practising, if you can avoid receivership, you do so. There are ways to work things out. You sit down with the owners and find a middle ground where you know they may no longer be in control of it."

Once again, the risk—of Olympic embarrassment or actual financial loss—had passed. As Bowra said, the world-leading example of environmental sustainability and excellent urban design was finished. The Maleks had delivered.

THE MALEKS, WHO had lost a fortune in the course of building an Olympic village, on time and to wide acclaim, and who struggled valiantly in the next three years to restore the health and profitability of their development company, were left to wonder how the City could be celebrating success while still leaving the impression that Millennium had failed. At the time, there were a number of theories as to what had gone wrong and who, actually, was at fault.

Theory number one is that the Maleks, a dark horse in the competition to develop the land, were in over their heads from the beginning—that they wanted the Olympic Village project too badly and that, in offering a $20-million premium over the next nearest bid, had paid too much for the land. Some of their competitors—which is to say, the people who lost out in the bidding—said as much at the time and it *was* an unprecedented price.

But before accepting any contention that the Maleks got the nod solely on the basis of a high bid, it's worth bearing in mind that the

City's Olympic Village vetting process came in two stages, including a first in which Millennium emerged on the short list of credible proponents because they had impressed the City with their proposal and design and had convincingly documented their capacity to execute the project well and on time. Yes, their price was right, but even more, the Maleks say, their plan best reflected the City's vision and ambition. Besides, on a $1-billion project, the extra $20 million in the Millennium proposal comes out as a rounding error. As the City's real estate lead Michael Flanigan has said, the Maleks were in no way naive. They knew how to value the land when they were making their bid, and they had a clear plan for achieving that level of valuation when the time came to put the product on the market. Looking at adjacent lands, it's also clear that those values were surpassed within the lifetime of the project—even despite the 2008 real estate meltdown. The project most assuredly did *not* suffer solely on the basis of a $20-million premium on the land purchase.

A second theory is that the project was simply too complicated—that it would have been better by far to continue the tower-and-podium/tower-in-the-park development style that had been so successful on the Expo 86 lands that Concord Pacific had developed on the North Shore of False Creek. Peter made that exact argument in one of Millennium's first meetings with the City, saying that, if the goal was to ensure the timely construction of good-quality housing for Olympic athletes—which could then be repurposed as condos and sold into a thriving market—the quickest, easiest, and most profitable approach would be to build four or five tall towers and cast the rest of that beautiful property as public green space. But the City had rejected that option even before calling for bids. Any of the proponents would have faced the same firm demand for a dense, relatively low-rise built form, clearly distinguished from the tall towers on the other side of the Creek. It's likely that every other developer would also have tried to convince the City to change its mind, and it's clear that they all would have run into the same determined resistance.

A third theory is that Millennium let the City push them around—in effect that the Maleks were too mild. You don't want to suggest this around Peter, who finds the notion offensive. There should, in any civilized exchange in society or business, be a distinction between decency and weakness. There is no question that the enthusiasts at Vancouver City Hall piled demand upon ambition upon even greater demand with the Olympic Village project, attaching a huge number of charges on the original project description and adding to those liabilities as construction unfolded. But even before the City started increasing its demands for green addenda, it was an indication that the politicians and the bureaucrats were determined to use the Olympic project to pay or deflect some big bills sitting on the City ledger.

The City also rewrote parts of the deal on the fly. For example, the original agreement called upon the successful proponent to assume responsibility for the security perimeter during the Olympic games, which seemed a reasonable request. But as the Games drew closer, the RCMP broadened that responsibility, announcing that the perimeter had to take into account the threat of sniper fire. That left Millennium having to stake neighbouring properties, paying for short-term leases from landowners who took full advantage of the fact that the Maleks couldn't walk away from a "negotiation."

Shahram, who keeps careful notes, still has the contracts showing what Millennium paid to both Wall Financial and Pinnacle Development for a two-month lease of two vacant lots: $250,000 each. These, again, were Olympic costs, ordered by the RCMP and the City of Vancouver and extracted from Millennium at a time when, in the words of Paul Merrick, "the City was the lender, the adjudicator and the review court." This was not a question of the Maleks being soft, Merrick says. In the post-2008 meltdown period, when the City had bought out Fortress and held all the cards, this was a matter of Vancouver politicians and bureaucrats taking advantage when Millennium had no choice but to comply.

Millennium construction manager Hank Jasper tallied these and other Olympic-related costs at the end of the project. On top of the late additions, the biggest cost was for the "exclusive use" period, after the project was built but before it could be occupied by buyers—a period during which the City was still charging Millennium full and exorbitant interest on the entire amount of their debt: Jasper calculated the exclusive-use cost to be a little over $18 million while the village was in the hands of VANOC and almost $20 million more on the time it took, after the Games, to retrofit the suites and make them ready for buyers. Add $15 million for the cost of that retrofit and for the various security-related expenses, plus over $20 million for "construction acceleration"—the contractor overtime and other costs that the City so freely approved—and you're getting up over $70 million, not counting $100 million in high-cost interest payments.

All that doesn't add up to the Maleks allowing the City to push them around. Certainly, the City pushed and their interference cost Millennium dearly. But the Maleks didn't stick around out of weakness. They promised to produce a great village for the Olympics and for the citizens of Vancouver, and they stayed at their desks to keep that promise.

A fourth theory, related to the third, is even more popular: that the City simply demanded too much in terms of green and sustainability features and that Millennium was too accommodating. Millennium Water—now Olympic Village—which was planned, executed, and delivered in thirty months—was so filled with groundbreaking sustainability features and technologies that it won the top international award as the greenest complete community development on the planet. Clearly, Millennium delivered an unprecedented and complex selection of green features and, the critics say, that *had* to be expensive.

There's more disagreement on this one—a stark division between the romantics and the pragmatists. Among the romantics, you'd have to include Merrick's partner Roger Bayley, who, with the City's former planner Scot Hein, is full of praise for Millennium, and especially Peter, for accommodating environmental innovations as long as they could be added within the budget.

Among the pragmatists, Hank Jasper did the math on what it cost to embed so many unprecedented and, often, unproven environmental innovations, and he came to almost $39 million, a heavy additional weight but not enough by itself to endanger the project. Also pragmatic on this count, Peter rejects any credit for being accommodating. Much as Millennium is committed to sustainability, he says, once the project was in full swing and the Gregor Robertson Vision team was dreaming up a new, greenest-city-in-the-world feature a week, the City was already firmly in place as the client, the regulator, and the financier—and their observer was ever in the building, nodding and smiling when some new demand fell on Millennium's shoulders. In many cases, the Maleks simply couldn't say no. Second, and Peter believes this is even more revealing, if you tally up all the sustainability features in the Olympic Village project and then look at all the projects, large or small, that have been built since, you'll find that no one has repeated them in the same way—anywhere. If this mix of experimental practices was actually a good idea, he says, surely someone else in an increasingly green construction and development world would have adopted the whole package.

You can certainly argue that a City administration, bent on building Vancouver's reputation as a global environmental leader, had every right to experiment with innovative features. It's hard, though, to argue that it should have carte blanche to dump the expenses for that green adventurism on a developer that was already moving mountains to hit an insanely ambitious construction deadline.

If you have a wonderful memory for numbers, or you regularly read with a calculator at hand, you'll notice that Jasper's estimates for soil remediation and extraneous Olympic and environmental expenses already add up to more than $120 million. And because he's a stickler for details, Jasper would also want you to know that Millennium also wound up absorbing another $20 million-plus in "accelerated tendering" costs—what they had to pay to contractors who knew they had Millennium pinned against an immovable deadline (and who enjoyed generous City support whenever they asked for more money to keep the pace). So, in addition to the long list of assets the City celebrated in its own final news release, that's a further $140-million value to City taxpayers that was extracted from Millennium—a number that might have been taken into account when the City seized the property because the Maleks were just 4 percent short on a $200-million loan repayment instalment.

The Maleks point out, as well, that they were never really credited with having been able to negotiate and execute a $10-million after-the-agreement purchase of a critical site within the village area. The so-called Sauder property sat on the northwest side of West 1st and Manitoba, a parcel the City had been unable to secure prior to the proposal call. Had the Maleks not been able to negotiate the purchase once work was underway, the project area would have been left with an undeveloped lot, likely a large surface parking lot, at the main entrance of the Village, instead of a well-integrated mixed-use block anchored by the TD Bank and featuring both social housing and market apartments. So, after speaking with Jody Andrews of the

Olympic Village Project Office, Shahram called and met with Ken Scott of Sauder Industries, the property owners, and negotiated the deal that had eluded the City. Then, perfectly accustomed to operating at warp speed, the Maleks got GBL architects working on plans to incorporate this crucial piece into the village. It added more work to be completed in the same time, and Shahram estimates that it also inflated their construction costs by tens of millions more, again for which they were not credited.

The Maleks' overarching answer to the question of what went wrong is to question the validity of the question itself. It's true that they were ambitious with the price they bid for the land. It's true that the village design was complicated and that the City never stopped piling demands upon the project, among which was an unprecedented and, according to Peter, a never-to-be-repeated suite of green features. But the Maleks still got it done, on time. And they say categorically, if the City had shown a modicum of patience and business acumen in late 2010, instead of pushing them out they would have paid out their loan without trashing the rest of their enterprise.

A related point, and it's one that the Maleks take personally, is whether the Olympic costs were ever "out of control." It's true that costs escalated—and escalated faster and with less discipline as the City imposed its will on Millennium. But it's a stretch to blame the Maleks for losing budget discipline when it was so often the City's observer who was approving or encouraging expenses.

In terms of Olympic-style cost control and value for money, it might also be worth comparing Millennium's project performance against the others building Olympic facilities at the same time—remembering that each of these came totally and exclusively out of the taxpayers' pockets. The Athletes' Village in Whistler was originally budgeted at $16 million and came in at $46 million, almost three times as much.

The Olympic Oval was originally budgeted at $60 million but was upgraded to $155 million because the City of Richmond wanted something more lavish and agreed to pay the bill—the ultimate cost: $178 million. The new Vancouver Convention Centre, a single structure that was built as a media centre for the Games, was budgeted at $500 million and came in at almost $900 million. By comparison, in 2009, Vision Vancouver, fresh off its election win, pegged the Olympic Village cost at $1 billion, but five years later celebrated its resolution by saying the City had covered the entirety of their $630 million in external debt, while also repaying in City working capital and recovering an additional $70 million.

In that light, the Maleks freely acknowledge that the project was challenging, and made more so by the 2008 financial crisis, not to mention the City's opening conditions and evolving demands. But even aside from the economic injury they suffered when the City pushed them out after the project's successful completion, they remain dismayed that there are still people who think the project was less than a world-class example of great city building.

"I ALWAYS SAID that Olympic Village would never be seen as a success until there were coffee cups littered in the square."

Marketing guru Bob Rennie is one of those people with whom, conversationally at least, you have to jog to keep up. His mind and his mouth both run at unmanageable speeds and not always in a straight line; sometimes you just have to wait until he circles back to explain the connection behind his last comment. This, though, is relatively obvious: in the first year of its life—after the success of the 2010 Olympics and before the City was using the development as evidence of its good governance and sharp financial acumen—Olympic Village was a lonely looking place, in great part because residents were just beginning to move in and work was being done to get the large stores ready to open to the public. Rennie, who had been selling the Olympic Village continuously since Millennium hired him for the project in 2008, imagined a village square so crowded with well-heeled, coffee-addicted Vancouverites that City crews wouldn't be able to empty the plentiful wastebaskets often enough. But in 2011 he could only imagine.

In the oft-repeated words of the developer/planner/commentator Michael Geller, the new neighbourhood was a "ghost town"—a term that rankled when Rennie heard it. He was on a panel at a Simon Fraser University event in 2011 when Geller stood up in the audience, not so much to ask a question as to list the failures of the project and the people who had planned it, and a generally patient and gracious Rennie snapped, "Let's not hold the autopsy while the body is still alive."

Ask him about the project today and Rennie erupts in righteous vindication. The people who "paid too much" for their condos in 2008 are afloat on a huge increase in value. The MLS Home Price Index shows that values in False Creek are 1.8 times higher in 2023 than they were in 2010, which is equal to the highest increase shown anywhere in Greater Vancouver. The erstwhile ghost town is now one of the hottest meeting places in the city, with steady streams of pedestrians and cyclists passing along the seawall, diners lounging on brew pub patios, and residents and visitors lining up at food trucks ringing the square. Despite everyone's best efforts, the odd coffee cup litters the square.

THE MALEKS KNOW what they had and what they lost at Olympic Village, and while that experience was ultimately more bitter than sweet, they are assuredly *not* in the market for sympathy. They are enormously proud of the project, of its planning and execution, and of the quality of the architecture. There are more than a dozen large condo buildings, as well as shops, market rental and social housing, and a state-of-the-art community centre, all designed and built in thirty months, and no two buildings are similar. Shahram says, "Every building is different. It doesn't look like it was all built at the same time or by the same people." No one will ever arrive on the doorstep and think that this busy, vibrant, sustainable, and inclusionary neighbourhood was done hurriedly and on a budget, just to house some Olympic athletes and meet the political goals of the day. Millennium Water/The Village on False Creek/Olympic Village—by whatever name, this development will stand the test of time, limestone and all.

In a definitive, if begrudging way, even the City of Vancouver finally acknowledged the Maleks' contribution. It came in a two-paragraph addendum in the same 2014 news release that announced the final interment of the Olympic Village deal. It said: "The Village, which is North America's first LEED Platinum community, was designed, developed and constructed by the Millennium Development Group led by Peter and Shahram Malek. The project was achieved in a record 30 months from commencement of construction to the opening of the 2010 Olympic Winter Games."

The City also provided a fact sheet, further describing the development's success. In the final analysis, the City said, Millennium had delivered:

- 1,100 housing units, 370 of which were "non-market"—i.e., publicly owned housing for low- or modest-income renters;

- a 45,000-square-foot LEED Platinum-certified, waterfront community centre; and

- a rehabilitated shoreline including a new habitat island, seawall, pedestrian bridge, and intertidal marine habitat.

Without actually saying thank you, the City further credited Millennium with having created underlying infrastructure or otherwise laying the groundwork for a total of:

- 6.5 million square feet of residential and commercial space that will eventually be home to 16,000 residents;

- three child-care centres (one of which was already in place); and

- 25.8 acres of open public space, including a new waterfront walkway, a public plaza, a new public art installation, and a community garden.

In the process, Millennium also hit several other City targets. Working with the Building Opportunities with Business (BOB) Inner-City Society, they created one hundred jobs, plus training, for disadvantaged people from the Downtown Eastside, and they created a $750,000 legacy fund for ongoing training and employment support. They also more than doubled the City's challenge target for buying materials and services from businesses in the inner city, ultimately spending more than $25 million in the Downtown Eastside.

As Michael Flanigan pointed out, "All of the service costs for Southeast False Creek were also capitalized into the first phase," which means that aside from getting Millennium to clean up the entire toxic site, the City had built the roads, water, and sewage lines for an area three times the size of Olympic Village and frontloaded the costs onto the Olympic project.

All of which leads to a final point of consensus: no other developer in the city has ever tackled a project this large, delivered this quickly, or carried off as much award hardware in the process. Concord Pacific built many more units on the north shore of False Creek, but it did so incrementally over more than thirty years, one or two buildings at a time, all pre-sold and conventionally financed. There was no similar burst of construction and no pressure to deliver every aspect of a new community all at the same time.

The most obvious comparable as a complete community built from scratch is probably UniverCity, the community on Burnaby Mountain that SFU Community Trust developed on behalf of Simon Fraser University. It's smaller—with a likely ultimate population of around nine thousand—and it was considerably less complicated, rising on a greenfield site and, again, built incrementally. Planning began in the late 1990s and construction has occurred over a six-teen- or seventeen-year time period. Final sales are expected in the mid-2020s.

Gordon Harris, who was president and CEO of the trust as it brought that project to fruition, says he is an unabashed admirer of the Maleks and an unwavering fan of their work. He says, "Like pretty much everything they've done, Olympic Village is beautifully conceived and expertly delivered. They did it on an impossible timeline, and even when everything was working against them, they behaved with absolute grace." Today, Harris says, "The village is a treasure. It's functional, livable, and more sustainable than almost any other neighbourhood in the region. It's remarkable—a credit to the Maleks and a lasting reminder of their commitment to doing the right thing."

In December 2014, after working for years to erase the Millennium name from every part of the development, the City of Vancouver finally agreed to mount a plaque on the site to celebrate the project and to acknowledge Millennium's contribution. Although the City initiated no fanfare, there is a lovely photo commemorating the moment when the plaque—with the design graciously gifted by Sheila

Henriques—was unveiled, with Peter and Shahram standing proudly on either side of their father, Amir, who had flown to Vancouver from Paris for the unveiling.

The full text, posted over the twin logos of Millennium and the City of Vancouver, and under the headline, Millennium Water Olympic Village, reads:

> North America's first LEED Platinum Community was developed and constructed by Peter and Shahram Malek's Millennium Development Group in time to open as the Athletes' Village for the successful Vancouver 2010 Olympic and Paralympic Winter Games.
>
> Formerly an industrial site, Millennium Water Olympic Village was the catalyst for the revitalization of the surrounding False Creek Neighbourhood and is a testament to the innovation, hard work and community spirit of the Malekyazdi family and hundreds of men and women who helped make this vision a reality.

If you tour the eight square blocks of the village with the brothers, they point out every feature, each chiming in on everything from the choice of tile or finishes to the evidence of architectural and planning excellence, inside and out. Even though the City blocked them from purchasing units after the handover, apparently again to prevent any public perception that the Maleks had somehow profited from their participation, it's clear that they still have a sense of ownership and enormous pride in a job well done.

Taken in that context, the Olympic Village story was not evidence of overreach or inexperience. It certainly isn't proof that the Maleks are somehow too *nice* to thrive in a sometimes-ruthless development world. (Looking at the brothers' body of work—and especially the award-winning projects they continue to produce today—they obviously have thrived.) Rather, they embraced the Olympic Village as a test of their skill—and a test of character. There were a couple of junctures when the Maleks could have stopped the work, called the lawyers, and held the City—and the Olympics—hostage. They could have tipped the project into bankruptcy and dragged the City into a long, expensive, and damaging court case. There also was at least one opportunity when they could merely have walked away, perhaps leaving their initial $29-million deposit—and another $25 million they paid to secure the funding before the Fortress retreat, together with other cash injections they made—but protecting all of the other assets that they had put up as security. But they had taken a job, and they were confident in their ability to complete it better than anyone else. So, they stayed. They did the right thing.

They are equally confident that, had they been allowed the scope and freedom to see the sales campaign through to its conclusion, they would have saved the City and themselves an additional fortune. They are certain that they would have done a better job for all concerned than a receiver who billed the City millions while the City was liquidating the Maleks' assets at whatever price could be fetched in time to tie up the paperwork—and put out the news release—before the next election.

In that context, Shahram pauses, reconsidering something he'd said earlier—his "I'd do it all again, even if I knew how it would turn out." Then again, he says, he can't imagine it turning out quite so badly on another occasion. He and Peter would certainly be more cautious, and despite this example, he would still expect more grace and honour from a municipal partner. Still, thinking about the effort that went into those frenetic years and about how much damage the brothers sustained, to their reputation as well as their fortune, he says, "It was an interesting experience, but very painful." Then he pauses again, because it is so obviously not in his nature to end on a negative, and he says, forcefully and conclusively: "But no, I don't have any regrets. We're proud of what we built and how we did it."

RESILIENCE

There is a morning-after metaphor—or maybe it's a cliché—about what happens when the dust settles after a cataclysmic event. It evokes that moment when you can take a clean breath and look into the future with clarity, if not confidence. But in the weeks and months after the City of Vancouver seized Millennium Water in 2010, the metaphorical air was still choked with debris. Strategically and temperamentally, the Maleks had always kept out of the limelight, pursuing the work and eschewing the attention. They were never the people playing politics in the backroom or speed-dialing reporters. Now, having spent three years with their names too frequently on the front page, they longed for a return to that lost anonymity. Fame had not brought happiness.

As the lawyer Neil Kornfeld noted, Millennium's unsolicited Olympian notoriety clouded their attempts at rebuilding. No lender was in a hurry to finance a new project, no matter how impressive the Malek track record or how promising the pro forma. The City had done a thorough job of finding and seizing everything the brothers might have used as collateral for raising new money. City lawyers had even insisted on a codicil (long since released) stating that if the Maleks were found to have concealed anything of value, the City could swoop in and confiscate that as well.

That wasn't going to be a problem. The City had also scuttled ten years' worth of ensuing work that had been sitting in Millennium's pipeline, including the mid-process projects on Evelyn Drive and on two large Lower Lonsdale waterfront properties, as well as a high-rise site in Brentwood that was tenanted by FedEx, and the high-rise site next to the Olympic Village. On top of the direct seizures, a decade of future work disappeared overnight.

The fallout was still worse. Wherever they went, people kept asking "But, isn't Millennium bankrupt?" The answer was an emphatic "No!" Receivers Ernst & Young put the shell company, SEFC, into bankruptcy in 2014—but that was four years after they had taken control from the Maleks.

Millennium never stopped. Peter and Shahram continued their activities, despite the turmoil, and they remain grateful to their core team, including Zul, Helena, Hank, Adam, Ryan, Max, Andy, Ben, Anthony, Gladys, Kerry, Reza, Iman, Pouya, Kelly, Kian, and Hazel. These staffers, many of whom remain with the company, ignored the negativity, proceeding like battle-hardened soldiers who could tackle anything after the Olympic Village experience. A testament to their dedication, they also took a voluntary salary cut to enable the company to weather the storm. Hank, who had worked so hard and fought the unfair barrage, moved on.

Throughout this period, the Maleks were touched to receive a host of letters and calls of support from unexpected quarters, some expressing indignation at the way they were treated by the City. Allan De Genova and Farid Rohani, now honorary colonel and honorary lieutenant-colonel respectively in the Canadian Army Reserves, were among those offering encouragement and asking how they could help.

Yet, there was a single property that still had potential—a prime site at the foot of Davie Street on Bidwell Street, barely a block from English Bay beach. This could be considered the apex of Vancouver's ever-popular West End, one of those high-traffic, high-profile, high-value locations that demand something special and promise a good return. But the Maleks were deemed to owe more on the property than could easily be recovered on a quick sale, which is why the City hadn't seized it with Millennium's other assets. Instead, the City attached a $5-million charge that would have to be paid before any redevelopment, a gesture that Peter says felt like "pure evil" at the time, calculated more to compromise their ability to get back on their feet than to allow the City to actually recover more money.

This became an interesting moment for the brothers to contemplate one of the great pieces of advice Amir had given them when they first arrived in Vancouver. Amir encouraged them to join the local industry association, the Urban Development Institute (UDI), arguing that they should take their place in the community and learn to work with their colleagues and their competitors. He argued that it wouldn't hurt in the good times and might help in the bad.

The previous three years had raised major doubts about Amir's optimism. Certainly, Rob Macdonald had spoken up for Millennium at a critical time, but UDI kept quiet as the City pushed the Olympic project to the brink. Some insiders added to the whisper campaign, saying that the brothers had been in over their heads, that they had paid too much for the land and that their organization was not large or strong enough to deliver such a complicated development, especially on such a short timeline. Some openly proposed to "rescue" the Olympic Village project, in what could easily be interpreted as a self-serving effort to push Millennium out and take over. As one of the UDI board members said to Shahram off the record: "They yak and yak because they are jealous of you."

After watching the Olympic Village takeover and, in some cases, lining up to buy some of the valuable properties the City had seized, a few developers came sniffing about the Davie-and-Bidwell parcel— but most were clearly looking for a bargain, not a partnership. The exception was Concord Pacific CEO Terry Hui.

The Concord Pacific website pitches the company as "Canada's largest community builder," and with its development of the 80-acre Expo lands on the north side of False Creek, and its huge CN Rail land project in downtown Toronto, it would be hard to argue the point. Concord Pacific had also been a finalist in the bid to develop Olympic Village, so if any Vancouver developer was going to be feeling competitive resentment for having been upstaged by Millennium, Terry Hui might have been a prominent candidate. But Shahram says that "Terry wrote a nice note when we were selected," and had been measured in his responses throughout the controversies that followed. "He never joined the bandwagon of critics, and in fact praised Millennium's efforts in building the Olympic Village."

Hui was interested in the Davie-and-Bidwell location, and he offered to buy the debt on the property, including the $5-million interest-bearing charge placed by the City, and accepted a 50-50 split on the development. Most important, Hui let Millennium be the developer. Peter says, "Concord never does that. They'd never done it before, and they haven't done it since." While Hui has a reputation for fierceness at the negotiating table and for insisting that Concord is always the sole lead on its many projects, Shahram says, "Terry was very gracious." At which, Peter chimes in to say, "It was a business deal. We made good money and Concord made good money. Concord was always fair."

For his part, Hui says there was nothing charitable in doing the deal—but he says so in the most charitable way. On one hand, he says, "It was a good project at a good location, and they offered me a good deal. They also build good stuff, so it just made sense." Hui says that he was one of many people who "recognized what Millennium had done for the city" at Olympic Village and that he, personally, loves the project. The Maleks "deserved a chance to rebuild their ship. They wanted to keep their team together," he says, adding that he understood that for Peter and Shahram, "this project would be a foundation to build on."

So, it was. Even as Ernst & Young was still managing sales at Olympic Village, the project now known as the Alexandra began to rise from the rubble as evidence of Millennium's resilience. It's an elegant tower, eighty-five luxurious homes and forty-nine market rental suites, all over street-level retail—and bundled beautifully in a LEED Gold-equivalent package. It affirmed for the Maleks themselves and for anyone else who was watching that they were still in business.

Early in 2012, even before the Alexandra was completed, however, the Maleks had noticed a For Sale sign on a Mazda car dealership, which they turned into a mixed-use project on East Hastings Street, at the base of the enduringly trendy Vancouver neighbourhood that the locals all refer to as "The Drive." Encouraged by the unfolding success with the Alexandra, the Maleks staked this project by mortgaging their children's apartments, and in a nod to the Bohemian feel of the neighbourhood, they christened it Boheme. Four storeys with 102 residences over 24,000 square feet of storefront commercial and office space, it was a typical Millennium development—practical, profitable, and noticeably nicer than anyone else might have built in the same location.

The next major project, in 2016, was a signature building in the rapidly expanding Burnaby neighbourhood of Brentwood—not far from where they had built three previous award-winning residential towers as part of their One Madison Avenue master-planned community. (The land for the fourth tower was taken by the City of Vancouver.) The new project, a 47-storey tower designed by award-winning Chris Dikeakos Architects (CDA) and marketed by the capable George Wong and his Magnum Projects team, was called Triomphe, and the title translates perfectly: after the struggle to get back on their feet, this landmark building is, indeed, a triumph—an architectural gateway to Brentwood, that, typical of the Millennium style, presents more like a five-star resort hotel than a residential tower. It has 340 luxurious one-, two-, and three-bedroom homes, as well as a row of townhouses at the base, all anchored by a 3-storey amenity building with a cantilevered facade and waterfall. It's a project that people remember.

When the mortgage advisor, Graham Thom, first asked how much money the Maleks were planning to put into the project, Shahram says he paused with embarrassment before saying, "None." It's the kind of answer they hadn't uttered since the days, decades earlier, when they were just breaking in, developing strip malls in the distant suburbs. But Thom knew who he was dealing with. He went on to help assemble the funding, including from Don Voth, former head of Metro-Can, showing his faith in the brothers after his work as one of two general contractors on the Olympic Village, as well as Grosvenor and Otéra Capital, the subsidiary of pension fund Caisse de dépôt et placement du Québec, which had financed several of Millennium's pre-Olympic projects in Burnaby and had almost financed the Olympic Village project itself. Despite early pessimism from Neil Kornfeld, it turned out the brothers' reputation, which the politicians had worked so hard to tarnish in the public mind, was still sufficient to win support in a couple of critically important corners.

But the project had its challenges getting off the ground. The land assembly was close to falling apart after one of the key vendors challenged its own joint owners' right to sell to Millennium and took Millennium and their own partners to court, despite the best efforts of Millennium to resolve the matter peacefully. After a long and expensive court process, where everything hung in the balance, the judge ultimately ruled in favour of Millennium and the development was able to proceed.

A big part of Brentwood's appeal is its convenience; Triomphe is a five-minute walk to the Gilmore station on the Millennium SkyTrain line. And yes, the name "Millennium" is entirely coincidental. If you go two stops down to the Holdom station, you get very close to the next Millennium project, another elegant three-tower residential development called Etoile, which Millennium initiated in 2018. Again designed by CDA and marketed by Magnum, this development defines the luxury market in this part of town, featuring three towers that are 26, 32, and 47 storeys. The first two towers stand over a sweeping porte cochère that fronts a four-level podium with a series of luxury townhomes and a full, flowing floor of amenities, and gardens.

Looking at all the work in Brentwood in the 2010s and 2020s, it would be overstating the case to call it a Millennium neighbourhood. But there's no question that it will be a better neighbourhood—more beautiful, more livable, more sustainable—because of Millennium's involvement.

"IT'S SHAHRAM'S FAULT. He likes these difficult, complicated projects."

When Peter says this, it's hard to tell if he's kidding, complaining, or actually encouraging his brother and business partner. Whichever the case, there is a ring of truth to the statement. It seems to be Shahram's role to fall in love with some seemingly impossible project, and Peter's job to help realize the vision—beautifully and at a profit. They clearly decided to test this theory at 1 West Hastings, a smaller project one can only term a labour of love, that the Maleks began in 2015.

At the time, 1 West Hastings was the address of the handsome but dangerously dilapidated Merchants Bank. When it was built in 1913—on what was then one of the most important corners in the twenty-seven-year-old City of Vancouver—the structure had been an imposing, neo-classical jewel. It was designed by American-born architects Woodruff Marbury Somervell and John L. Putnam, whose other prominent Vancouver buildings include the Birks Building that once stood at Granville and West Georgia and the Seymour Building, a 10-storey neo-Gothic office tower that was, for a brief time, the tallest building in Vancouver.

From the granite base to the Corinthian capital, 1 West Hastings had been designed from the outset to express solidity and prosperity. It was wrapped in a better-than-limestone andesite, quarried from Haddington Island in Broughton Strait, near the tip of Vancouver Island. Haddington andesite is the same cladding that was used on the Hotel Vancouver and the British Columbia Legislature, admired for its beauty and beloved by artisans for being easy to cut and carve. Just 3 storeys tall, the Merchants Bank steel-and-concrete core was designed to accommodate an additional four to seven floors and, in the words of a thirty-two-page Conservation Plan that the City of Vancouver demanded when Millennium proposed a redevelopment, the interior "was outfitted with the most lavish materials available."

By 2016, however, Merchants Bank—the business—had been gone for almost a century, and Merchants Bank—the building— was a broken shell, with a collapsing roof, three feet of water in the basement and a facade cloaked in hoarding to prevent injury from chunks of stone that were breaking off and falling to the sidewalk below. Even the pawnshop (the building's last successful tenant) had long since gone out of business. But the Maleks had been driving past Merchants Bank for years and they had always loved it. "The building is absolutely beautiful," Peter says, "and very unique in Vancouver." Both Maleks say they are saddened by the gorgeous heritage struc- tures that this young city has lost already. They mention the second Hotel Vancouver, as well as the old Pantages Theatre, a Downtown Eastside treasure that also slipped into disuse and was demolished in 2011 after its roof collapsed. Even the more grand, stately Majestic Theatre, which sat directly across the street from the Merchants Bank, had been levelled to make room for surface parking. Against this his- tory, the Merchants Bank seemed worth saving and when the For Sale sign went up, it took Shahram no time to call the listing agents about making an offer.

The shambolic state of the structure was only part of the problem. For those not familiar with this part of Vancouver, West Hastings at Carrall Street is pretty much ground zero in the city's fragile Downtown Eastside. The neighbourhood is frequently dismissed as being dysfunctional, but Gordon Price says that's neither accu- rate nor fair. Price, who was a Vancouver city councillor from 1986 until 2002 and later founded the continuing education CITY pro- gram at Simon Fraser University, says the Downtown Eastside may be crowded with vulnerable citizens, but it is also an efficient service centre for that same population. It contains the densest concentration of social housing and single-room-occupancy hotels, as well as a large assortment of social services and outreach agencies. Canada's first safe injection site for intravenous drug users is just a block and a half from 1 West Hastings. It's true the neighbourhood has one of Vancouver's highest rates of petty—and sometimes violent—crime, and whether you're walking the streets or driving by in your car, you can't ignore the poverty and misfortune laid bare in one of the richest cities and countries in the world. But, Price says, the police, the politicians, and nervous homeowners and businesses in adjacent neighbourhoods are all perfectly satisfied not to poke what many believe to be a hornet's nest of trouble. They would rather keep the people and the problems of the Downtown Eastside kettled in a small area than do anything to push them farther afield, where they might unsettle a different group of neighbours. Price says, "It's all about stability," and some in the community worry that any effort to renovate or revitalize such a critical corner could be destabilizing.

The people of the neighbourhood are also protective of their space—and they are particularly jealous of the space adjacent to Merchants Bank: the smallest park in Vancouver at 0.03 of a hectare, which is formally called Pioneer Square but popularly known as Pigeon Park. It's more of a plaza than a park. When the bank was built, there was still a train track running at the diagonal in front of the building, and when the train service was cancelled and the tracks were ripped up, there remained a tiny triangle in a dense neighbourhood that has little other room to gather. As described in the alternative weekly, the *Georgia Straight*, "Pigeon Park has long served as a living room for low-income earners and people who live in the Downtown Eastside without a roof over their head." It's generally busy, and while the scene might look rough to the bourgeois passersby, there is a strong sense of community among the regulars. When a group of entrepreneurs opened the high-end PiDGiN restaurant across the street in 2013, some local agitators rose up in protest, screaming about the displacing effects of gentrification and denouncing well-heeled restaurant goers as poverty tourists and voyeurs.

Larry Beasley, the former co-director of planning at the City of Vancouver and a long-time friend and fan of the Maleks, picks up the story: "When the Maleks started talking about a restoration, both the City and the Parks Board basically told them to ..."—well, it's a gritty euphemism for "go away." The bureaucrats seemed to consider the site just too much trouble.

But the Maleks say that's not how it went. When they first contemplated purchasing the property, they found the City of Vancouver Heritage Department to be supportive, almost enthusiastic. The brothers left the first discussion thinking that they could preserve the building and add several floors. And, if they could secure the adjacent property, they might also be able to create a larger mixed-use project that would help a restoration make sense economically as well as socially.

So, they went ahead and bought the bank building, together with an adjoining property on Carrall Street, housing the disintegrating shell of the old Bijou Theatre, an early cinema that went out of business during the 1919 flu pandemic and was repurposed, repeatedly and roughly, for the next eighty or ninety years. Next, they purchased the adjacent McConnell Block, which was built in 1889. A mixed-use office building of just 2 storeys, it was later converted to become the Louvre Hotel and, later still, the Gospel Mission. In a 2018 report that made the case for its restoration, the consultants at Donald Luxton & Associates said, "The heritage value of the McConnell Block lies in the historic relationship between Gastown and the economy of early Vancouver." Reading between the lines, you might reasonably conclude that the building had no inherent heritage value whatsoever.

The entire ground-floor facade had been removed and much of the rest of the building was falling down. There being little to actually restore, the McConnell needed to be rebuilt almost from scratch.

This is the moment when a less-stubborn landholder might start praying for a small, geographically specific earthquake, for certainly it would have been more efficient—and a great deal less expensive— to nudge everything into a pile of rubble and begin again. Instead, the Maleks set about the most loving restoration. They stabilized and restored what was left of the McConnell facade even while commissioning a brand-new structure in behind that bridged the empty space and married it to the restored Merchants Bank. The City rejected any suggestion that Millennium should be able to realize the original architect's dreams of a taller building on the Hastings Street corner. Against every good argument, historical or economic, City staff conceded only a single additional storey—which they further demanded be set back, out of sight from the street. The City then slammed a height limit on the McConnell side, as well; although the zoning allowed for a rental building of up to 12 storeys and the usually tough Gastown Historic Area Planning Committee offered support for a taller building, Vancouver's planners said, arbitrarily, that Millennium could go only to 7, erasing the potential for forty additional rental units in a market in dire need of housing.

Undeterred, the brothers designed a wonderfully practical plan to repurpose the whole property as an elegantly modest boutique hotel, one that could provide employment to the very people you might otherwise find loitering in Pigeon Park. Millennium has a good track record in the hotel world: L'Hermitage on Richards Street emerged after the Olympic Village debacle as one of the company's great and enduring successes. The Maleks also had an extremely positive experience during the Olympic Village construction with recruiting and training new employees from among the otherwise hard-to-employ residents of the inner city. During the thirty-month burst of construction, and in keeping with their father's long-standing tradition of corporate philanthropy, Millennium worked, to everyone's benefit, with the Building Opportunities with Business Inner-City Society, helping dozens of people who had been considered unemployable to join the ranks of reliable and steadily employed construction workers. A hotel on the site of the McConnell Block and the former Louvre Hotel seemed like an obvious place to reprise such a program. Again, however, it was not obvious to the City. And, to add one last component to the situational inertia, the Vancouver Parks Board rebuffed every entreaty to work together to put more energy (or money!) into Pigeon Park.

Of course, the dour prophets at the City and the Parks Board were right to anticipate a certain amount of pre-loaded outrage, which burst forth immediately upon Millennium launching its first round of advertising for prospective tenants for the renovated Merchants Bank. The mere mention of a building "restored to its former elegance" triggered a caustic reaction, with eastside activist and writer Karen Ward decrying the project as "aggressively gentrifying." In a critical outburst in the *Georgia Straight*, she said, "This is not displacement; it's an attempt to erase that history in a very comprehensive, in a very complete way." Ward didn't explain how salvaging one of the few century-old buildings still surviving in Vancouver could constitute a "comprehensive" assault on the city's history.

This was about the time Larry Beasley stepped back into the picture. "I was worried for them," he says. He met with the Maleks and toured the now-bustling site, and he could see they had spared no expense in the quality of the restoration. But he could also see that "every indicator was telling them they shouldn't be doing this." So,

Beasley assembled a small group of advisors to come up with innovative ideas for what could be done at the park and for businesses and tenants that might succeed, and that would be supportive rather than disruptive, in the community. Beasley also suggested that the brothers contact Constance Barnes to help connect them even more deeply to the Downtown Eastside community.

Barnes is a can't-help-herself kind of activist. She's the daughter of Emery Barnes, the larger-than-life former NFL and CFL football player who in 1972 became one of the first two black Members of the BC Legislature and, later, the first black Speaker in any provincial legislature in the country. Emery Barnes had been a social worker before his political career, and while the Downtown Eastside was just outside the boundaries of his own constituency, he was always a reliable friend to those in need. Constance followed in his footsteps—into politics, on the Vancouver Parks Board from 2008 to 2012, and as a compulsive fixer and conciliator in the inner city.

By the time Beasley was encouraging the Maleks to reach out, Shahram had already made the connection. Barnes was running the weekly pop-up Downtown Eastside Street Market and needed money for fencing and tables, and she found that the Maleks were both generous and sincerely interested in the fate of the neighbourhood. She called up old contacts at the Parks Board to help open a dialogue and she connected the brothers to Skundaal Bernie Williams, the Haida carver whose Survivors' Totem Pole was raised in Pigeon Park in 2016. All are continuing to work to protect the condition of the pole in the future.

As the project unfolded, Barnes encouraged the Maleks to stick with their plans to hire and train locals. Barnes says, "They're very open. They just keep asking, 'How do we make this work?'" She also says that she believes they're in it for the long term. "They've been respectful on a level that's not just about revenue. It's about history and a long-term commitment to what they're doing."

Looking at the properties now, the new and restored structures, and the extraordinary attention to detail, it is hard to imagine a short-term business case for the project. The site needed to be extensively re-engineered, requiring a huge amount of reinforcement and concrete work to accommodate new entryway layouts, new stairs, and a link to a new elevator—all necessary to conform to the modern BC Building Code.

The main staircase of the Merchants Bank, for example, was both a dream and a nightmare. It is exquisite: the smooth marble treads rise in a tight turn, such that no two corner stairs are exactly the same in shape or dimension. It's absolutely not the kind of feature that could be produced—or even repaired—on an assembly line. But, in an A-list heritage building, the staircase is also a substantial and ceremonial feature, and the decorative wrought ironwork on the balusters alone was clearly too precious to abandon. Even after a century of neglect, that iron was robust and recoverable, but the same couldn't be said for what was left of the wooden banister, which was so rotted and broken that the pieces couldn't even be used as a template for a replacement. For that, the Maleks found Wally Zacharias of Zimal Homes. Zacharias is a seventy-three-year-old craftsman who worked on his first Gastown project when he was just seventeen—that's a fifty-six-year span for those who don't want to do the math. He opened his own shop thirty-five years ago and decided to specialize in staircases, in part because few others were up to the challenge. In the carpentry world, even a straight staircase is unforgiving: you're working in three dimensions and tiny errors accumulate as you go. But Zacharias and his crew welcome the curves, twists, or spirals: "When it gets too hard, that's where we like it."

The Merchants Bank project gave them a lot to like. Thanks to the standardization of the modern Building Code, most staircases have regular shapes. If Zacharias and crew are fashioning a new banister—or even restoring one in a younger building—they take the measurements, set up their equipment, and cut all the pieces in short order. They usually complete even a complicated, 4-storey banister in sixteen to twenty hours. Zacharias's senior assistant, Steele Mallat, says the Merchants Bank took "a couple of hundred hours." In addition to being irregular in shape, the straight-grain oak banister is almost 5 inches in diameter, so every piece was oversized and all the connecting joints had to be hand-carved. Then, because 5 inches is impractically huge for the average person's hand, they also had to build a second, standard 1.5-inch handrail, so people will have something convenient to hold on to.

The finished product is magnificent—it's the kind of luxurious detail you'd expect in the office of a lawyer whose services you can't afford. You can imagine interior designers and antique aficionados dropping in just for the pleasure of running their hands along the broad, silky-smooth finish and saying, "They just don't build 'em like this anymore." And with the rarest exceptions, they don't, because it's just too expensive. In 1913, the still-prosperous executives at Merchants Bank paid $100,000 for the whole, beautiful building. When Zacharias considered bidding on other parts of this project, he figured that his price just for replacing the Merchants Bank windows would exceed that amount.

Peter confirms that it was expensive to restore the double-hung, one-over-one, wooden sash windows—especially the ones that are bowed—"but not *that* expensive." Still, while touring the building, Shahram pointed out a single new interior window that alone cost one-tenth of the original construction price for the whole building.

The window was added to share light between buildings and to allow people on the floor of the former bank building to see the complicated and beautiful staircase. But Building Code required that the window also be rated to provide fire separation—hence, $10,000 for glass alone.

Looking again at the whole spectacular project and reviewing the original question of whether the brothers should have taken it on or walked away, Larry Beasley says, "It's a conundrum. The setting is unbelievably challenging, and the building was so fragile. But the Maleks had the courage to do it." He speculated that the brothers "have a vision for the neighbourhood" not as a place to gentrify, but as a historic precinct worthy of long-term investment. "And I think they're right," Beasley says. Even while he was still at the City of Vancouver as the co-director of planning, he too dreamed of a brighter future for this troubled but historically rich district, and he ran into the same resistance—the same fear of displacing a vulnerable population or being accused of gentrification.

Regardless of Peter's jocular opening—despite his comment that starting this complicated project was "Shahram's fault"—Beasley says, "I think they talked one another into it. I think they were romanced by the building." Beasley says that, as much as Shahram likes a complicated and beautiful project, Peter, the engineer, "loves the puzzle." And just looking at how the three properties are now woven together physically—and how they might ultimately function economically—you can see both the complexity of the puzzle and the creativity of the solution.

Beasley also says that "every developer tends to have a pet project, something to feed their creative need." For example, Polygon's Michael Audain has invested a huge amount in art—as has marketing guru Bob Rennie. Looking at the artistic and creative expression that the Maleks have delivered in the restoration at 1 West Hastings, Beasley says, "I'm almost jealous of their capacity to take on a project like that."

Beasley suggests that there is something altruistic in the brothers' work on this complicated corner. "They think they can assist—and not displace." Constance Barnes agrees, saying, "You might want to call it gentrification, but you might want to call it giving back to the community. They're very open to saying, 'How do we make this work?'" And, she adds, they have risen generously whenever she has leaned on them for donations.

The inclination to help runs in the family: Amir Malek was always a quiet philanthropist. When he set up a charitable foundation, he named it not for himself but for the city of his birth, and he continued to donate, and to invest in community, long after he was forced to abandon his original fortune in Iran. In that way, you might consider the restoration of 1 West Hastings—this precious, irreplaceable architectural treasure—as another gift to the city, even if it was one that the skittish politicians and bureaucrats of Vancouver City Hall resisted at every turn.

NEW OPPORTUNITIES

"This is the story of this country. It's the immigrant story."

The speaker here is Paul Merrick, who was born in West Vancouver in 1938, the year the Guinness family finished the Lions Gate Bridge. Merrick says it's worth remembering that, with the exception of the Indigenous population, "we're all immigrants." And new immigrants often bring such gifts—their energy and their dreams, their intelligence, and their expertise. Amir Malek brought a young family, including two sons who, though still in their twenties, were already well-tested in the development world. Merrick says, "I always got the impression that Amir was giving his sons as much rope as he could. He was trying to get them out there, and he did."

Indeed, Shahram says that, even though one brother trained in engineering and the other in business, Amir wanted both of his boys to have the capacity to do their own work. "It's why he gave us responsibility for our own projects. And the partnership with Peter works well for this reason."

Which raises an interesting question: How does it work? How is it, working a lifetime with your brother?

Shahram's answer could seem evasive were it not so revealing. He says, "We were all trained by our father, and when in doubt we always ask ourselves how he would have done something. And since our father gave us the opportunity to manage our own companies, from a fairly young age we were each responsible for all aspects of real estate development and construction on large-scale projects from A to Z. Reporting to our father as the group chairman, our sole motivation was to work for the betterment of the family organization, in an honest and effective manner. He wouldn't expect anything less. So personal issues never came into the picture."

Amir also told all of his children that, if they had differences, they must resolve them among themselves and never complain about another sibling, inside or outside of the family.

You can see today how well they work together, how they leverage that sibling energy. Peter and Shahram are both sticklers for detail, endlessly holding one another to account, checking their facts, and questioning their assumptions. And if they don't always agree right away, Shahram says, "We always talk it through and finally wind up with the best solution."

The comment about keeping family complaints in-house is also a wonderful reminder that Amir Malek was not one of those disengaged workaholics who set a bracing example but left parenting to others. This is a man who thought deeply about every aspect of his life, who made rules and shared strategies for success. This is a father who would take the time to edit the letters of a homesick nine-year-old—even then, imparting the wisdom that everything worth doing is worth doing well.

After he successfully launched his sons in Vancouver in the early 1980s, Amir returned to Paris—which, next to Tehran, was his wife's great love—and, at age seventy, started the European development operation that his advisors had warned would be impossible. Working almost until his death in 2019, at age ninety-eight, he initiated a raft of construction work, as well as twenty-five major development projects—nineteen residential and six mixed-use—in the neighbourhoods around Paris. It's no wonder that one of the questions Shahram and Peter so frequently ask one another is, "How would Dad have done it?"

Another question that the brothers seem to have worked through, in a practical if not philosophical way, is: What does it mean to be a developer? Peter and Shahram describe it as a variation on being builders, i.e., people who are in the construction industry. Where a building contractor takes a commission, the developer takes the risk, perhaps for a higher reward, perhaps not. They also take enormous pride in conceiving and designing beautiful, practical things, but (even if not always successfully) they have always tried to stay away from the political and often belligerent debates over the role and character of developers.

Given how many people seem to hold a hostile view toward the development community, that may be no surprise. There is no shortage of critics who disparage developers as rapacious and relentlessly cost-conscious puppet masters, ever on the lookout for a hot deal and consumed with squeezing the greatest profit out of every transaction. In this characterization, the nature or even quality of the product seems almost incidental. In these circles, the word "developer" itself is almost a pejorative.

At the other end of the continuum is a notion of the developer that would be analogous to an auteur in the film world, someone who manages a collaborative project so well that it lifts the whole enterprise to the status of art. In film, the auteur—usually the director—is managing actors and technicians to bring to life the potential of a script. But there is more to the process. Someone has to measure the potential, consider the public mood and marketability of "the property." They have to round up the talent and, critically, secure the financing.

It's oddly similar in development. There is an architectural script that can't find true expression—or, really, any expression—without a veritable battalion of workers and other resources. The auteur—in this case, the developer—has to find a suitable space in the market and round up the money.

I put those two definitions to Ian Gillespie, who, as the principal of Westbank Corp, is famously resistant to calling himself a developer, even if the top hit on the Internet leads to the Westbank website and offers the description: "Canada's leading luxury residential and mixed-use real estate development company." Gillespie's low opinion of many of the people in his business is immediately evident. He says, "Most people's impression of a developer is probably right. Just because you can play a few chords, that doesn't make you a guitar player. It certainly doesn't make you an artist."

But Gillespie says the hostile view of the developer is still "grossly unfair" to many of his colleagues and competitors. He also says that, within the mixed development community, the Maleks are special. "I think of them as city builders."

The difference, he says, is a matter of approach. One is purely transactional; the other is longer term. "It's a more thoughtful, historical approach as to what's your role." And the latter requires "a degree of humility." Gillespie says, "We're only here for a moment in time. It's a matter of how you judge success, of asking yourself, when you look back on this moment in fifty years if you'll be proud."

Looking at the Maleks' body of work, Gillespie says, "I'd say they did it right."

The Maleks have certainly approached development as a craft, beginning by acquiring the technical understanding you need to do it well. Recalling the words of Metro-Can's Don Voth, it's what enables Peter to "go toe to toe with any contractor," fully comprehending the details and implications of every aspect of the work.

They also expanded their capacity with every new project. From construction and into development, they worked their way, literally, toward the task that Ian Gillespie describes as "city building." They became specialists at creating whole neighbourhoods, including City-in-the-Park, St. Andrews at Deer Lake, the One Madison Avenue towers in Burnaby, and culminating with what surely must be acknowledged as a magnum opus at Olympic Village. Consider that, at City-in-the-Park, they built seven towers in sixteen years; at Olympic Village, they built twelve towers in thirty months.

Ask them now which was their favourite of all these projects and—perhaps surprisingly, perhaps not—the first thing they mention is Olympic Village. Notwithstanding the painful parts, it is a stunning success: Gary Mason, the *Globe and Mail* columnist whose scoop precipitated much of the Maleks' trouble with the City, and who continued for years as a trenchant critic of the project, looked back in a 2014 article and wrote, "The Olympic Village now is one of the most enviable residential districts in the city—albeit one with a notable and inglorious past." It's beautiful, functional—a global example of livability and sustainability. It's also a feat that is unlikely ever to be duplicated. As Peter says, "It takes longer today to get a permit for a single building than it took us to build the whole project."

But "Olympic Village" was the reflexive answer. As the brothers consider the favourite-project question further, Peter says, "It's a little like asking, who is your favourite child?" And then they fall into a lengthy reverie, bringing up one building after another: the Stern buildings in West Vancouver (Edgewater and Water's Edge); Lumiere in downtown Vancouver, where Peter lives now; the seven-tower City-in-the-Park community; Triomphe, the Etoile towers. They wax lyrical about the lovingly restored Province Building and the classical beauty of 1 West Hastings, into which they moved their own offices in 2023. And in every reference, they skip over the grandeur of the success to talk instead about the granularity of the process—and especially about the seemingly insurmountable obstacles that emerge in the midst of every project. As Larry Beasley said, talking about how energized Peter became in working through the technical challenges on the Merchants Bank project, both brothers clearly love the puzzle.

Addressing the Millennium legacy, and perhaps especially the breadth of their contribution, Shahram says, "If you build the same thing over and over, it's easier to make money, but I think we have more fun. We really love Vancouver and want to preserve its history and make a meaningful contribution to the city and the country. We also take pride when other developers do something special; we get excited about that as well."

LOOKING BACK ON all the Millennium projects, and on the intimate familial affection—and effectiveness—of the Maleks' lifelong partnership, it seems too early to write a book like this. First, it's too soon to pass the enterprise on to the next generation of talented people—which they intend to do.

Having righted the ship that was damaged so badly, and so unnecessarily, after the Olympic success, the Maleks have nothing more to prove and no urgent need to expand their empire or their wealth.

But there are puzzles yet unsolved. The city of their dreams is not yet finished. There are big, sweeping, multi-building projects like their Burnaby development Etoile, with its final 47-storey tower that will stand as the culmination of another luxurious trilogy, this time accommodating rental and affordable housing as well. There are projects that others might find impossibly complicated, like Millennium Central Lonsdale. A handsome mixed-use, residential/retail/medical/office building at 13th and Lonsdale in North Vancouver, it will also serve as a podium for an 18-storey tower, housing 162 condominium suites that, again, will be among the most luxurious the North Shore suburb has yet seen. Designed by Chris Dikeakos Architects, the building boasts sweeping views, north to the mountains and south over Burrard Inlet and the city of Vancouver, as well as a location that can't be matched for its convenience and proximity to every imaginable shop or service—or hospital: Lions Gate is only a block away. The excellent location was actually one of the most difficult complications in getting the project off the ground. Tenants in the former building, including the main North Shore licensing office of the Insurance Corporation of BC, loved the spot and were in no hurry to move. Millennium wound up finding a new site on Marine Drive in North Vancouver and building a turnkey operation with more than twice as much space as an inducement for ICBC to move.

The Maleks being the Maleks, however, the work plan would never be complete without something even more complicated—and more obviously a labour of love. How else could you describe the tiny two-building renovation at Barclay and Nicola in Vancouver's dense, residential West End? The buildings, dating from 1924, look like two big homes that were joined and converted into shops with apartments above. While they are on the City of Vancouver's Heritage B-list, you wouldn't necessarily have thought them as architecturally

splendid—or even salvageable—when the Maleks bought the property in 2020. The corner building was sagging badly at one end,
which, on inspection. was easily explained: there was no foundation.
It was just a wooden building sitting on the shifting ground. It also
housed an old corner grocery, where the proprietor had fashioned a
unique cooling system for his big chest refrigerator: he just ran cold
water through it 24/7. Even aside from the obvious waste of that
method, when the Maleks checked the bills, they realized the landlord
had been paying the City more for water than it had been collecting
in rent from the grocer.

Given the density of the neighbourhood—there's a 15-storey
tower across the street—and the need for housing in Vancouver, it
seemed an obvious place for another modest mixed-use building
incorporating the heritage structure at its base. But the City greeted
every such proposal with a flat "no". Despite the lost opportunity, the
Maleks embarked on a careful restoration, lifting the corner building to fill in the foundation and working through the offices, shops,
and apartments to bring everything to a modern standard, while still
respecting the line and form of the 1920s original design. The result
is destined to be a neighbourhood treasure—the kind of thing that
will be even more difficult to redevelop in the future because people
love it too much. And as such, it's the kind of project that a developer
would do only out of a sense of citizenship—and because they enjoy
the work too much.

Mahin Malek has lately been urging her industrious sons to contemplate an easier life. Peter says, "Our mother says, 'You should
slow down,'" and because she is their mother, they acknowledge her
opinion. But they also remember their father, who said, "The biggest
recreation is work." The man who, having left Iran, having helped his
sons and daughters establish their own business in Canada, returned

to Paris and started afresh, pursuing his own passion for creation for two more decades.

So, yes, the brothers acknowledge their mother's view, but the company is in such great shape and there are so many opportunities still awaiting. In fact, Shahram says, "Yes, and there is this land assembly...," and Peter smiles.

There is much more to come.

REFERENCES

Adab, Fred. Personal interview with the author, November 30, 2020

Ashley, Terry. "Timeline: The Evolution of the 2010 Olympic Budget," *Global News*, February 11, 2009, https://globalnews.ca /news/70997/timeline-the-evolution-of-the-2010-olympic-budget/

Ballem, Penny. Email communications with the author, July 8, 2021

Barnes, Constance. Personal interview with the author, June 10, 2021

Bayley, Roger. *The Challenge Series*. Roger Bayley Inc., 2009

Bayley, Roger. Personal interview with the author, November 17, 2020

Bayne, Ken. Personal interview with the author, November 27, 2020

Beasley, Larry. Personal interview with the author, November 25, 2020

Brook, Chuck. Personal interview with the author, February 26, 2021

Bucher, J. "Penny Ballem, City Manager, City of Vancouver," *BC Business*, April 21, 2009, www.bcbusiness.ca/penny-ballem-city -manager-city-of-vancouver

Bula, Frances. "Olympic Village: The Cost of Green Design + Why Millennium Was Chosen," State of Vancouver: Frances Bula on City Life and Politics, January 11, 2009, www.francesbula.com /uncategorized/olympic-village-the-cost-of-green-design-why -millennium-was-chosen/#disqus_thread

Bula, Frances. Personal interview with the author, November 5, 2020

Bula, Frances. "Vancouver Takes Control of Olympic Village," *Globe and Mail*, November 17, 2010, www.theglobeandmail.com/news /british-columbia/vancouver-takes-control-of-olympic-village /article1461654/

Burgmann, Tamsyn. "Prices Slashed Up to 50% for Olympic Village Condos," *Globe and Mail*, February 17, 2011, www.theglobeandmail.com/news/british-columbia/prices-slashed -up-to-50-for-olympic-village-condos/article566884/

Canadian Press. "Olympic Village Goes into Receivership," *CBC News*, November 17, 2010, www.cbc.ca/news/canada/british-colum-bia/olympic-village-goes-into-receivership-1.891836

Chung, Phil. Personal interview with the author, December 9, 2020

Cooper, Sam. "City of Vancouver Taxpayers Facing Upwards of $300-million Loss on Olympic Village: Expert," *The Province*, July 30, 2013, https://theprovince.com/news/vancouver/city-of-vancouver -taxpayers-facing-upwards-of-300-million-loss-on-olympic-village-expert

Cutler, Mark. Personal interview with the author, November 18, 2020

Dawson, Yvonne. Personal interview with the author, February 17, 2021

Doyle, Larry. Personal interview with the author, February 4, 2021

"Final Sale of Olympic Village Wins Gold for Vancouver Taxpayers," News Release; City of Vancouver, April 28, 2014, retrievable at www.vancouverisawesome.com/courier-archive/news/updated-city -of-vancouver-sells-final-stake-in-olympic-village-2977152

"First Olympic Briefing Closed to Public, Robertson Says," *CBC News*, December 9, 2009, www.cbc.ca/news/canada/british -columbia/first-olympic-village-briefing-closed-to-public -robertson-1.761820

Flanigan, Michael. Personal interview with the author, November 24, 2020

Geller, Michael. Personal interview with the author, January 29, 2021

Gillespie, Ian. Personal Interview with the author, February 11, 2021

Harris, Gordon. Personal interview with the author, March 7, 2021

Hein, Scot. Personal interview with the author, November 25, 2020

Howell, Mike. "Updated: City of Vancouver Sells Final Stake in Olympic Village," Vancouver Is Awesome, April 28, 2014, www.vancouverisawesome.com/courier-archive/news/updated-city -of-vancouver-sells-final-stake-in-olympic-village-2977152

Hui, Terry. Personal interview with the author, February 11, 2021

Jasper, Hank. Personal interview with the author, November 18 & 19, 2020

Keenan, Hayden. Personal interview with the author, October 22, 2020

Ladner, Peter. Personal interview with the author, November 13, 2020

Lee, Jeff. "In Olympic Village Debt Being Paid Off, Vancouver Politics Is Alive and Well," *Vancouver Sun*, April 28, 2014, https://vancouversun.com/news/staff-blogs/in-olympic-village-debt -being-paid-off-vancouver-politics-is-alive-and-well

Lupick, Travis. "Restaurant Patio Proposed for Pigeon Park Pits Developer Against Activists," *Georgia Straight*, January 9, 2018, www.straight.com/news/1015846/restaurant-patio-proposed -pigeon-park-pits-developer-against-activists

Lyon, Stu. Personal interview with the author, February 2, 2021

Macdonald, Rob. "How the City Messed Up Millennium Water," Vancouver Sun, October 16, 2010

Mackie, John. "What Vancouver Needs 'Is a Tiny Bit of Grit,'" *Vancouver Sun*, September 9, 2006

Mackin, Bob. "The Olympic Village Developer Is Bankrupt," TheTyee.ca, April 5, 2014, https://thetyee.ca/News/2014/04/05 /Olympic-Village-Developer-Bankrupt/

Malek, Amir. "Autobiography," unpublished manuscript, 1993

Mason, Gary. "Millennium Speaks, Says the Job Will Get Done," *Globe and Mail*, January 20, 2009, www.theglobeandmail.com /news/british-columbia/millennium-speaks-says-the-job-will-get -done/article1152030/

Mason, Gary. "Olympic Village Proves to Be a Costly Lesson for Vancouver," *Globe and Mail*, April 29, 2014, www.theglobeandmail .com/news/british-columbia/olympic-village-proves-to-be-a-costly -lesson-for-vancouver/article18317203/

Mason, Gary. Personal interview with the author, March 2, 2021

Mason, Gary. "2010 Games: City's Deal with Developer: CFO Had Every Right to Question Vancouver's Olympic Village Loan," *Globe and Mail*, November 11, 2008

Mason, Gary. "Vancouver Looks to Borrow $800-million," *Globe and Mail*, January 17, 2009, www.theglobeandmail.com/news/british -columbia/vancouver-looks-to-borrow-800-million/article1152029/

Maurice, Helena. Personal interview with the author, November 24, 2020

McCarthy, William P.J. "The Failed Experiment of Vancouver's 2010 Olympic Village," *Real Estate Issues* vol. 37, nos. 2 & 3 (2012), www.google.com/url?sa=t&rct=j&q=&esrc=s&source=web&cd =&ved=2ahUKEwjSxcOV14eBAxViADQIHcUcD-oQFnoEC-BgQAQ&url=https%3A%2F%2Fcre.org%2Fwp-content%2Fup-loads%2F2017%2F04%2F37_2_3_Vancouver_Olympics.pdf&us-g=AOvVaw0JmDQWa9mdrnuTfU17H4Gw&opi=89978449

Merrick, Paul. Personal interview with the author, March 12, 2021

"Olympic-sized Bailout," Macleans.ca, January 12, 2009, https://macleans.ca/general/olympic-sized-bailout/

"Olympic Village Chronology of Events and Community Benefits," City of Vancouver, April 28, 2014, www.google.com/url?sa=t&rct=-j&q=&esrc=s&source=web&cd=&ved=2ahUKEwiK18y42oeBAx-VmCTQIHWEzBzQQFnoECBoQAQ&url=https%3A%2F%2Fvan-couver.ca%2Fdocs%2Fsefc%2Folympic-village-fact-sheet.pdf&usg =AOvVaw13cOTLomqBxN5FVW3b4TqL&opi=89978449

"Olympic Village Developer Shahram Malek Talks about His Company's Legacy," *Georgia Straight*, May 13, 2014, www.straight.com /news/643726/olympic-village-developer-shahram-malek-talks-about -his-companys-legacy

"Olympic Village Loan Decision Unanimous: Ladner," *CBC News*, November 9, 2008, https://bc.ctvnews.ca/olympic-village-loan-deci- sion-unanimous-ladner-1.340751?cache=yes%3FclipId%3D104059

Price, Gordon. Personal interview with the author, March 10, 2021

Rennie, Bob. Personal interview with the author, January 25, 2021

"Robert Macdonald: Olympic Mess Is Nothing to Celebrate," *The Province*, September 9, 2014, https://theprovince.com/opinion /robert-macdonald-olympic-village-mess-is-nothing-to-celebrate

Rogers, Judy. Personal interview with the author, March 17, 2021

St. Denis, Jen, and O'Brien, Frank. "Anatomy of a Deal: The Sale of Vancouver's Olympic Village," Vancouver Is Awesome, October 9, 2014, www.vancouverisawesome.com/courier-archive/news/anatomy -of-a-deal-the-sale-of-vancouvers-olympic-village-2986717

Sullivan, Sam. Personal interview with the author, November 17, 2020

"Vancouver's Olympic Village: Let the Bailout Games Begin," *Time*, 2010, https://content.time.com/time/specials/packages/article /0,28804,1963484_1963490_1963439,00.html

Voth, Don. Personal interview with the author, October 29, 2021

"What's Really Happening in B.C.'s Development World?" *CBC News*, November 11, 2008, https://bc.ctvnews.ca/what-s-really-hap- pening-in-b-c-s-development-world-1.336514?cache=yes%3Fclip- Id%3D104059

"With Olympic Village Debt Repaid, City's Economic Position Even Stronger, Says Mayor," City of Vancouver, April 28, 2014, retrievable at www.vancouverisawesome.com/courier-archive /news/updated-city-of-vancouver-sells-final-stake-in-olympic -village-2977152

INDEX

ABOUT THE AUTHOR

Richard Littlemore is an author, journalist, speechwriter, and consultant who specializes in issues including urban planning and development, academic affairs, sustainability, and climate change. Recent books include: *Building Community: Defining, Designing, Developing UniverCity*, for Gordon Harris (with whom he is also writing the upcoming *Urban Waste Land*); *The Fight for Beauty*, and five other volumes for Westbank developer Ian Gillespie; and the award-winning *Climate Cover-up*, for former David Suzuki Foundation chair James Hoggan. Originally a newspaper reporter and editor (*The Ottawa Citizen*, *The Vancouver Sun*), Littlemore later served as an elected director on the Board of Metro Vancouver, as a writer and advisor to governments at all three levels, and as a speechwriter to the leading university presidents in BC and Alberta. He lives, works, and rides his bicycle (a lot) in Vancouver, BC.